NOW they make it legal

Reflections of an aging Baby Boomer

By Howard Harrison

First published by Dog Ear Publishing
4011 Vincennes Rd
Indianapolis, IN 46268
www.dogearpublishing.net

ISBN: 978-1-4575-4272-5

This book is printed on acid-free paper.

Printed in the United States of America

Stories

Prologue

McDonald's. Fish sticks. Disneyland. Coke in cans. These are just some of the American institutions that debuted the year I was born, 1955.

Legos and Velcro also were invented that year. Guinness published its first book of world records. Bill Gates and Steve Jobs were born. And, in December, just weeks before my birth, a black woman, Rosa Parks, refused to give up her seat to a white man on a bus in Alabama – and many people cheered.

I was born into what would surely be an era of progress and enlightenment. The country was proud and confident. We'd just trounced the Nazis and the Japs (no longer politically correct, I know) in World War II, ending things abruptly in 1945 with our unveiling of the nuclear bomb.

Upon returning home, U.S. soldiers found a country about to experience unprecedented economic prosperity. They got jobs, married and built houses in the suburbs. Our dads worked; our moms had babies.

In 1957, U.S. births reached a record 4,300. That year, the U.S. government defined people born between 1946 and 1964 as "baby boomers." Nearly 80 million babies were born in the

United States during those 18 years, more than had ever been born before or since in any period of our history. By 1964, Baby Boomers made up 40 percent of the U.S. population. We still make up about 25 percent today.

My sisters, born in 1945 and 1948, are what are sometimes called Early Boomers. People born in the late '50s and early '60s are sometimes called Late Boomers. I'm right in the middle, although I relate more to the Early Boomers. One indicator is if you remember the JFK assassination or were eligible for the draft during the Vietnam War. If you don't or weren't, you're a Late Boomer.

To say I am an aging Baby Boomer is really redundant because if you are a Baby Boomer at all, and you're alive, you're aging, or aged. The youngest of us have turned 50 while our oldest members are pushing 70. We will soon become the largest group of welfare recipients in U.S. history. Our sheer numbers threaten the solvency of Social Security and Medicare.

We had great ideals. "Make love, not war." We had a level of social consciousness that the "older generation," i.e., our parents, didn't have. We would make the world a better place.

Did we succeed? Frankly, I'm a little disappointed.

Marijuana is just now becoming legal in some states and is still illegal in most. Are you kidding me? Four and a half decades after Woodstock and we still haven't gotten this done?

I had hoped that by now we would have progressed enough as a civilization to make war closer to obsolete. I thought by 2015 countries would have found better ways to settle differences than still seeing who can kill the most people.

Remember when we made going to the moon so common-place that it became downright boring in the 1970s? I thought we'd be colonizing planets by now.

But my purpose is not to criticize. It is to re-examine and reflect while I still have all my marbles. Because let's face it, Boomers: our best days are behind us.

"Back in the day" we didn't have cell phones, kids. There was no Internet. There were no video games. We rode bikes without helmets and in cars without seat belts while our parents chain-smoked with the windows rolled up.

Somehow, some of us have lived to tell about it. So sit back, relax, take a toke if you're still into that sort of thing, and allow me to reminisce. It was a great ride. You just may not remember much of it. Perhaps I can help jog your memory.

Mercurochrome

I was born on December 22, 1955. My mother went into labor during a late-night poker game and delivered me Thursday morning around 4 a.m. at Michael Reese Hospital in Chicago.

For the first five years of my life, I lived with my parents and two older sisters on the first floor of a duplex, or "two-flat," in Skokie, Illinois, an older suburb just north of Chicago. Back then, Skokie billed itself as "the world's largest village." I never knew if this was actually true. Skokie's population was about 60,000 at the time. I think they banked on no one ever fact-checking the claim.

More than half of Skokie's population was Jewish. This included many Holocaust survivors and relatives of Holocaust victims. Some people may remember Skokie for the 1981 TV movie of the same name about a proposed neo-Nazi march through the village.

Our neighbors upstairs were somehow related to Jerry Stiller, the comedic actor. He was best known then as part of the husband-and-wife comedy team Stiller and Meara. I remember watching them on the *Ed Sullivan Show*. Today he is better known for his roles on the sit-coms *Seinfeld* and *King of Queens*, and as the father of actor Ben Stiller.

I never met Jerry Stiller, who played Frank Costanza, father of George Costanza (played by Jason Alexander) on *Seinfeld*. However, I did get to know Jason Alexander's real-life parents years later, in the 1980s. Alex and Ruth Greenspan (Jason Alexander's original last name) had a place in Florida right next to my parents. I'd see them when I visited my folks and they'd talk endlessly about their son being in some Broadway play, or a McDonald's commercial, or some sit-com pilot.

We'd go, "yeah, yeah," trying to be polite while our eyes glazed over – like their son was really going to be a big star or something.

One time after college, before I was married, I went to my parents' place with a couple of my buddies when my parents weren't there. Our intent was to party, go to some strip clubs, party, laze by the pool, and party – not necessarily in that order. Ruth, who was a nurse, was out of town at some convention, leaving Alex all alone. He clearly was not used to being alone.

He wanted to hang out with us. One day he offered to take us to breakfast. We were fine with this until he showed up at our door at 7 a.m., which was only a few hours after we'd gone to bed.

"What is it, Yom Kippur?" he yelled. "You're not eating?"

Another day he invited us over for a barbeque. "Have another frank," he kept insisting no matter how many we ate. Then he brought out dessert: a huge stick of pepperoni from which he began slicing huge hunks and forced us to eat them until our stomachs were bursting.

Yes, Alex was quite a guy. Ruth was even funnier. And their son became the greatest character in sit-com history.

Like many Baby Boomers, I was born to parents who grew up during the Great Depression and were now enjoying the affluence of America's burgeoning middle class in the 1950s. Their parents were Eastern European immigrants who came to this country in the early 1900s looking for a better life and to escape religious persecution.

My sisters were quite a bit older than me – 10 and 7-1/2 years, respectively. My father grew up on the north side of Chicago. My mother grew up in Duluth, Minnesota. My Aunt Tootsie was cousins with Bob Dylan, who was also from Duluth.

We Baby Boomers were the first generation to grow up with television. Maybe that's why I think of the first five years of my life as "the black and white years." TV was strictly black-and-white then. *Bonanza* became the first network TV show to be broadcast in color in 1960.

While my memories from the 1950s are cloudy, I have a few. I remember seeing the Oscar Mayer "Weinermobile" in downtown Skokie once. That was a big deal. (It must have been if I still remember it.)

I have vague memories of my family celebrating the Chicago White Sox winning the American League pennant in 1959. I remember my oldest sister singing a song about Luis Aparicio, her favorite player. I would become a huge baseball fan later in life, but I was just 3-1/2 years old when the Sox won the pennant in '59. I don't think I even knew what baseball was.

Rock and roll got popular in the late 1950s, led by Elvis, of course. Growing up with two older sisters, I had an early indoctrination to this new art form.

Also in the late '50s, iconic toys like Barbie dolls and hula-hoops were introduced. Passenger jets debuted. The space age began. The microchip was developed. Alaska and Hawaii became states. Castro took over Cuba. Other than the hula-hoops, I was oblivious to all of this.

Ironically, one of my earliest memories from the black-and-white years involves a product known for its bright red color. Remember Mercurochrome?

If you are a Boomer, you must, since our moms (or my mom at least) seemed to slather it on every nick, scrape and cut we got, and there were many when we were growing up. You'd cower in anticipation of her applying this shit, not so much because it stung, but because the bright red color made it *look* like it *had* to sting.

For the record, Mercurochrome was an over-the-counter anti-septic that contained mercury. Mercury came under scrutiny by the U.S. Food and Drug Administration in the late 1970s as a potentially harmful additive to drugs and other products. Mercurochrome was banned from the marketplace in the 1980s. But when we were growing up, Mercurochrome flowed like beer at Octoberfest.

Our two-flat had a back yard, which, since we lived on the first floor, was basically ours. One day I was running in the yard and fell, as little boys are prone to do. It hurt my balls, my testicles, also not uncommon. For you women out there, it feels like a hard punch in the gut, only lower and much more painful. The pain literally leaps into your throat and you are rendered senseless. (How's that, guys?)

The mistake I made was crying like a baby about it to my mom. The next thing I knew, I was on my back on a cold steel examining table with my pants down while our family pediatrician examined my balls. Then he told my mom I needed a hernia operation.

To this day, I don't think I needed a hernia operation. It didn't even hurt anymore – the pain had long since subsided. Naturally I winced when the doctor squeezed my balls. Who wouldn't? But you didn't question your family doctor. I mean, these guys actually made house calls. How embarrassing was that when you were just pretending to be sick to miss school?

Our pediatrician was your prototypical middle-aged, graying-at-the-temples, long-established community doctor that everyone brought their kids to. It might as well have been God saying I needed a hernia operation. I had my tonsils out a couple years later for the same reason. But then, didn't we all? Are there any Boomers out there that still have their tonsils?

The surgery would be done at Michael Reese Hospital in Chicago, where I had been born just a few years earlier. There were fewer hospitals in those days. Skokie didn't get its own hospital until a few years later.

I remember the hard rubber ether mask coming down on my face as they told me to count to 10. It was the most frightening experience of my life. (Okay, I was three years old, it was still traumatic). The odor of the ether and force of the mask being pushed down was suffocating. I was probably unconscious by the count of five but those were some harrowing five seconds.

The next thing I remember is sitting in a waiting room at Michael Reese listening to the song "Moon River" by Andy Williams playing over the loudspeaker. To this day, whenever I hear that song, I think of Michael Reese and my hernia operation.

I was bandaged from my naval to my knees when my parents took me home from the hospital. When they took off the bandages, the entire area was painted bright red. It was Mercurochrome. I screamed. I mean, at that point, I'm not sure I even knew what it was. Seeing that whole area in bright red shocked me. I just screamed over my red legs.

Side note: Around this time, the Cincinnati Reds baseball team began calling itself the Cincinnati Red Legs because this was during the Cold War and the word "Reds" was virtually synonymous with the word "Communists." People wondered, "What the hell does 'Red Legs' mean?" Well, I could have told them.

If you've never heard of Mercurochrome, you're not a Boomer. Just a taste of what life was like in the olden days.

The Five-and-Dime

J ust down the block from our house was the local "five-and-dime." While the name implies that everything cost a nickel or a dime, this was not the case in the late 1950s. Still, stuff was pretty cheap, especially candy. That's what I went there for. Giant (to someone under age 5) glass bins of every kind of candy imaginable lined the front window of the store. Cost per piece was probably a penny. Rock candy was my favorite. It looked like glaciers – made of pure sugar.

My local five-and-dime was like a small drug store. The grand-daddy of the five-and-dime stores – F.W. Woolworth Company – had a much broader assortment of merchandise. They even had lunch counters. But five-and-dimes were central in people's lives. This was before there were large pharmacy, convenience or department store chains on every corner.

My mom called our local five-and-dime "the dime store." "I have to go to the dime store," she'd say. Or I'd say, "Mom, I'm going to the dime store," when I'd walk or pedal my tricycle to the end of the block to spend my whole allowance on candy. They were also called "five-and-ten-cent stores" or "five-and-tens."

My most memorable experience at our local five-and-dime was when I spilled "Lik-M-Aid" in my eye. Lik-M-Aid was flavored granulated sugar that came in bright colors and was packed in a narrow paper tube, like a straw. You tore open one end, tipped your head back, and poured the sweet, tangy powder into your mouth. One time, I tore open the end, tipped my head back, and instead of pouring it into my mouth, I missed and poured it into my eye. I was certain I would go blind.

Next door to the five-and-ten was Marv's Barber Shop. It was a two-chair barber shop. There was Marv and one other barber. My mother always made sure I got Marv when she took me there to get my hair cut.

Crew cuts were the norm for boys under age five in the 1950s, so maybe I actually did get my hair cut as often as it seems like I did. Anyway, each time I did, my mom gave Marv $3, cash. It was the first time I saw how an adult made money. I decided right then I wanted to be a barber. It seemed like something I could do and was the only way I could understand at that point how you made money.

But the five-and-dime – I'll always remember the candy.

In addition to rock candy and Lik-M-Aid, other favorites of mine included "buttons," those little round multicolored candies that came stuck on a long paper sheet. You couldn't peel them off without a little of the paper getting stuck on the bottom of each one. But they were so good you'd eat them paper and all.

They also had those little wax bottles filled with sweet liquid. You bit off the wax top of each bottle (I can still taste the wax) to get a drink. I don't know what the liquid was. It tasted like warm Kool-Aid but sweeter. I felt like there was never enough liquid for how much wax made up the bottle.

I liked those candy bracelets – candies on a round elastic band. Girls might wear the bracelets for a time. I just ate off the candies.

I liked Pez, although as a kid the dispensers were the best part. I know I had a Popeye one and many others I don't remember specifically. Getting a new Pez dispenser was like getting a new toy more than just getting candy. I had no preference as to the colors and flavors of the little candy tablets. Was there a difference? If there was, I didn't notice or care. I cared more about the dispenser.

Of course, we all enjoyed candy and bubble-gum cigarettes. They looked just like real cigarettes. They were sold in packs, with real brand names like Kent, Viceroy, Pall Mall and Lucky Strike, over the counter to four-year-olds like me, who then pretended to smoke them like our parents.

The candy cigarettes tasted like peppermint. The bubblegum cigarettes were wrapped in white paper to resemble cigarettes but you had to peel off the paper to get to the gum. Of course, you left it on for a bit while you pretended to smoke.

Kids' love of candy probably hasn't changed since we bought ours at the five-and-dime. But you don't see candy cigarettes anymore unless it's through some obscure vintage-candy merchant. We are much more protective of our kids today.

I was just a few years old when my parents let me ride my tricycle down the block to the five-and-dime. Most parents wouldn't let a three-year-old do that today.

Times were simpler. Was it more dangerous? Perhaps. So, why did it seem safer?

Sometimes ignorance is bliss. But not as much as rock candy.

Smile! You're on Candid Camera!

Who sends a four-year-old kid to day camp – on a bus, by himself, with all the other kids at least several years older? My parents, that's who.

I don't remember any girls at this camp, just boys. Maybe it was an all-boys camp? There were no age groups. All the boys, from me through kids who could have been as old as 12, did the same activities.

I cried every day except one. I remember this because I remember coming home one day declaring proudly, "I didn't cry today!" I don't remember being picked on as much as I always seemed to be afraid of many of the things we'd do in camp.

One day we were going canoeing. There were two teenage counselors. I had a choice of which counselor to go with. One had the worst body odor I'd ever smelled in my young life. I held my breath around him. The other was an asshole who actually joined the other kids in tormenting me. I thought for sure they'd throw me overboard. Without hesitation, I went with the smelly guy.

The camp had a swimming pool and while I did not know how to swim, I changed into my trunks each day and waded in the shallow end. I don't remember the camp trying to teach me to swim. That came at my next day camp. But I remember the clubhouse where we changed.

As we got naked, the older kids would point to a naked kid and say, "Smile. You're on Candid Camera." I was not yet familiar with the TV show *Candid Camera*, where they would set up funny situations and film people "caught in the act of being themselves." When the victim was thoroughly humiliated or frustrated, the host would pop out from behind the camera and say, "Smile! You're on Candid Camera."

Based on the way the term was being used in the clubhouse, I thought "candid camera" meant being naked. One time one of the younger kids – he was maybe seven – was pointing at me while I was naked, saying, "Look, he's camera camera, guys. That kid's camera camera!" This kid was too stupid to even say "candid" camera – this is what I was dealing with.

Anyway, one evening some weeks later I was home in my bedroom and my mom comes in and tells me there is a TV show on that she thought I'd find funny. It was called "Candid Camera."

I couldn't believe it. How does my mom know about "candid camera?" I thought that was just from camp. She's really going to let me see naked people?

That's what I thought I was going to see. I was disappointed. But *Candid Camera* became one of my favorite shows for years. Remember host Alan Funt? You can still picture him, can't you?

What a great show; one of the funniest ever. Wasn't it?

King Zor Versus Robot Commando

Growing up with two older sisters was almost like growing up an only child. They were both teenagers by the time I was five. So I played alone a lot. I enjoyed playing alone. It was less stress. You didn't have to share or get along with other kids. I could make up my own games and get absorbed in my own world.

We played with "real" toys. No microchips, video screens, virtual this or smart that. We had to use our imaginations a lot. I probably spent as many hours playing with my baseball cards (that's right, playing with them, not putting them in plastic sleeves so I could sell them someday) as kids today spend on electronic devices.

A pack of baseball cards cost a nickel. You got five cards plus a hard rectangular strip of pink bubble gum, which I usually threw away. I hated when some of the sugar from the gum would rub off onto the card it was next to. I grouped my cards by team and made up a way to play games with them. I played entire seasons, keeping score of the games and maintaining standings.

For the games, I arranged the cards in the "field" (the floor) by position, creating a makeshift baseball diamond. I'd roll a marble from the pitcher's card and hit it with the card of the guy on the other team that was "batting." I made up ground rules for what was an out, hit, double, triple or homer. I hummed the national anthem before the start of the game and the theme from *Exodus* during pitching changes, trying to sound like an organ. I did play-by-play and simulated crowd noise. My sisters made fun of me mercilessly. Can you blame them?

Toys were a big deal to us Baby Boomers. Of course, there weren't as many as there are today. I played with most of the standard toys of the day: Lincoln Logs, Play Dough, Pick-Up Stix, Silly Putty, Cootie … I never actually knew how to play Cootie but I assembled the bugs and had fights with them. I had Slinkys, which always seemed to get tangled beyond repair.

For some reason I always had an Etch-A-Sketch even though I never liked it. I could never maneuver that little pencil tip up, down or side to side with the two dials well enough to draw anything I was pleased with. It all had to be straight angles. It was hard to make curves. I didn't have the patience.

We had Mister Potato Head, which required a real potato. The set just came with the eyes, ears and other facial features to stick into the potato. When the potato starting growing things from its pores it was time to throw it away.

I played with Match Box cars. Most of them only cost 50 cents, although some were a little more. When the movie *Goldfinger* came out in the Sixties, I got the James Bond Match Box car, complete with ejector seat and other features.

NOW THEY MAKE IT LEGAL

Toy soldiers were big. There were different sets you could get
– U.S. Army soldiers, Battle of Iwo Jima, Charge of the Light
Brigade and others. I had the Civil War set, which came with
something like 100 blue (Union) soldiers and 100 gray (Con-
federate) soldiers, plus horses, canons and other accessories.
There were crawling soldiers, soldiers with legs spread to sit
atop the horses, crouching soldiers and soldiers standing
upright and poised to fire.

I would spend hours setting up the battle scenes: this soldier
under the coffee table, these guys behind the couch, others
riding in on horseback out of the bathroom, snipers hiding
behind throw pillows. It then took about 10 seconds to wipe
out all 200 soldiers and start again.

I loved View Master. You can keep your high def. Those plastic dual-lens hand-held "projectors" that looked like binocu-
lars showed the crispest, most detailed 3D images any of us
had ever seen when you'd insert the circular picture cards. I
had many sets although the only one I remember for sure was
Bambi.

I also enjoyed Colorforms. I guess they still make Colorforms
and View Masters, but I'm sure they're not as popular today. I
loved the flat, rubber characters and accessories you'd get in a
set, which you'd stick onto a shiny, colorful board that provided the physical environment.

The first licensed Colorforms character was Popeye. I had
many other Colorforms sets over the years but Popeye was my
first favorite super hero. I once made my mom buy me a can
of spinach so I could eat it like Popeye did. One taste did away
with that practice, however.

One of my earliest toys that I remember – I was probably around three – was a wind-up car that had a flat, die-cast metal Popeye attached to the bottom. When you wound it up, Popeye would lift the car over his head, put it down, lift it over his head again and so on until it stopped and you had to wind it up again.

When we brought this toy home from the toy store, I went straight to my room, wound it up and put it on the ground. Popeye began to lift the car, but instead of flipping it over his head like he'd done in the store, he stopped mid-lift and the car sank back to its original position. I kept trying and the same thing kept happening.

I had a major tantrum. I was screaming, "I want it to work! I want it to work!" I was crying hysterically. I would not stop. My mother told me we'd go back to the store tomorrow and get a new one. "I want it to work NOW!" I demanded at the top of my lungs. I would accept nothing less.

Seriously, having since had kids of my own, I cannot believe my mother's patience. I don't remember either of my kids ever having a tantrum like this.

Finally my mom reached her breaking point. She burst into my room, picked up the car, grabbed the die-cast Popeye, and began twisting it violently until it completely broke off. Blood was streaming down her wrist.

You thought I was screaming before? Now I picked it up a few octaves. "I want a toy!!" I screamed. "I want a TOY!!" I screamed it over and over again.

I don't remember how it was resolved. I probably cried myself to sleep or my dad came home and taught me a lesson with "the strap" (his belt).

My all-time favorite toy was King Zor. I started seeing commercials for it while we still lived in our old house during Saturday morning cartoons. The Christmas I got it we'd just moved to our new house, so I was five or six.

King Zor was a large (almost kid-size) green plastic dinosaur. He ran on regular "D" batteries (no Alkaline back then), as did most toys, flashlights, radios and other gadgets. He had a long tail with a round target on its tip, and he came with a dart gun that shot plastic projectiles with suction cups at the end.

When you turned him on, King Zor began moving forward slowly and steadily, making a low rumbling sound. The idea then was to shoot a dart at his tail. When you hit it, he'd turn around toward you, the volume and ferocity of his growl would increase, and he'd shoot a projectile from his mouth back at you.

This thing would be so outlawed today. The number of potential risks it posed to a small child would make product-liability attorneys' heads spin. But that was then and this is now, if you know what I mean.

King Zor was my favorite toy despite the fact that I associate him with the moment I realized there was no Santa Claus. It was my first Christmas in the new house and I still believed in Santa when I saw King Zor standing out among all the other unwrapped toys in front of the fireplace Christmas morning.

(My mom never wrapped my Hanukah/Christmas presents when I was growing up.)

The thing is, only my mom knew how badly I wanted King Zor. As I looked at the other toys, they too were things I'd told my mom, and only my mom, that I wanted. I suddenly figured out who Santa Claus was. I just suddenly went, "Duh."

King Zor was followed the next year by a similar toy called Robot Commando. The only difference between it and King Zor was that it was a robot instead of a dinosaur and the projectile he shot back at you came from his head versus his mouth.

I eventually broke both toys but continued to play with them manually. I had more fun having them battle each other by hand than I did when they could move on their own and you'd shoot darts at them. They had some real knock-down, drag-outs until they both were completely demolished.

School Daze

As I mentioned, when I was five, we moved to a new house – a four-bedroom, three-bath free-standing split-level in a newer area of Skokie. It was a half-block from the school where I would start kindergarten in the fall of 1961.

The neighborhood had a lot of young families with kids. I had virtually no friends in our old neighborhood. Still, the move was initially upsetting.

My parents had taken me to the new house several times over the past year while it was being built but I guess it never registered with me that we would actually be moving there. Then one day my mom takes me there, only this time we're there a real long time. I was tired and bored. I was five. I wanted to go home.

"But we are home," my mother said. I will never forget those words. Shock waves went through my body. I had no idea. You mean we're not going back to our other house, ever? I have to *sleep here*? I might as well have been kidnaped by strangers – that's how foreign it felt.

Of course, I soon got used to the new house and it became our family home for the rest of my childhood. Being a half-block from school, I was a "walker." Kindergarten was a half-day. I went mornings. I was home by noon, in time to watch *Bozo* on TV while I ate my lunch.

When I started first grade, school became full days. Throughout grade school, I usually had the hot lunch in the cafeteria. Thirty-five cents got you a plastic tray with four or five compartments of food items – like a TV dinner – plus a small carton of milk.

I rarely went home for lunch even though I lived close enough. I never brought a sack lunch either. Sack lunches reminded me of day camp, an annual ritual for about a half-dozen summers during my childhood that I absolutely abhorred.

I was a good student in grade school, although my behavior took a little turn beginning in fourth grade. I once had to write 100 sentences two days in a row and have them signed by my parents. The first day it was "I will not interrupt the Pledge of Allegiance," which I think I negotiated down to "I will not interrupt the Pledge." The next day it was the popular "I will not talk in class."

It was also in fourth grade that I began shoplifting baseball cards and other items from Walgreen's, Woolworth's and other fine retail outlets – until I got caught. I was with my friend in a department store called Turnstyle. I was shopping for a Father's Day gift for my dad. There was a bottle of Brut cologne for $5 and a bottle of Old Spice for $3.50. I wanted to get my dad the Brut.

As I had seen my dad do many times, I removed the price tag from the more expensive item and replaced it with the price tag from the cheaper item. There were no bar codes or scanners in those days. The cashier simply rang up the price on the paper sticker affixed to the item.

As soon as the transaction was complete, a burly store detective grabbed my arm. My friend and I were taken to a back room and they called our moms to pick us up. My friend's mom got there first. He told her that he didn't do anything, which was true. I was the one that did it. He was just with me.

"Do you know that if you're with someone who commits *murder*, you are as guilty as the person who commits the MURDER!" my friend's mom screamed.

Then my mom got there. First I denied I did anything, claiming the wrong price tag was already on the Brut and I was the victim of some incredible miscarriage of justice. At some point on the ride home I finally owned up to it.

"Wait till your father gets home," I was told. And that was scary, because my dad didn't get mad very often, but when he did, he could be frightening. He had a booming voice and a rough background. Let's just say he'd done much worse things than change price tags in his day.

The thing is, as I said, I'd seen my dad do exactly what I did many times. At the hardware store and other places I'd go with him, he'd routinely switch price tags.

So I'm up in my bedroom sweating it out when I hear my dad come home. Then I hear him coming up the stairs. It was a good life while it lasted, I thought.

Then he walks in. "Your mother told me what you did," he said in his deep voice with a stern face. "I just have one thing to say to you." Pause. I'm waiting for him to hit me or something. "I'm glad you got me the more expensive cologne."

That was it. I'd been reprieved. I learned later from my sisters that my mom was much angrier at my dad than she was at me. She blamed him for the whole thing, told him it was his fault. I really didn't think so. I knew what he was doing was wrong and I knew it was wrong for me to do it. But maybe it did make it seem more acceptable to me, at least subconsciously.

Either way, since that incident, I have never again taken anything that didn't belong to me. At first it was because I didn't want to get caught again, but eventually I came to believe that stealing is one of those absolute wrongs, like killing or hurting people. I don't believe in a lot of hard and fast rules in life but those are the two I gave my kids: You don't hurt people and you don't take shit that doesn't belong to you.

At least I learned something while I was in grade school.

We Bring You This Program in Living Color

Baby Boomers are the first generation to grow up with television. When my oldest sister was born in late 1945, only about 7,000 U.S. homes had TVs. When I was born in 1955, television was pretty well established. By 1960, nine of 10 U.S. households had televisions. Most of these, of course, were black-and-white.

For most of us Boomers, it is hard to imagine life without television. Those who can remember are becoming increasingly scarce. The fact that I think of my first five years as "the black and white years" shows the influence of television on how I view my life.

Before 1960, virtually all TV shows were in black-and-white. One of my favorite shows during the black-and-white years was *Captain Kangaroo*, which was on weekday mornings. I am told that I watched it sitting on the floor in front of the TV in my pajamas while eating my morning cereal.

I loved Hanna Barbara cartoons such as *Huckleberry Hound* and *Yogi Bear*. I also remember watching *Leave it to Beaver* on Saturday nights while still living in the old house. I wished my parents were more like Ward and June Cleaver, who'd sit down and talk to their kids with empathy and understanding about morality and other life lessons. That was definitely not my parents – nor, I suspect, yours.

In the early '60s, I became addicted to sit-coms like *Lucy, Andy Griffith* and the *Dick Van Dyke Show*. They were still in black-and-white but would switch to color later in the decade – except for *Dick Van Dyke*, which went off the air after the 1966 season before it was to convert to color.

The first time I saw color TV was in the early to mid-1960s at a motel in Minneapolis. My cousin was getting married. I was there with my family for the wedding. Late one night, we were in my cousin's motel room and the TV was turned on to *The Tonight Show* with Johnny Carson. The picture wasn't the greatest but it was in color, which was very cool.

We got our own color TV shortly after that. It was a 25-inch console with remote control. The remote control in those days actually turned the dial on the TV to change channels. My only disappointment was that most shows still were in black-and-white. *Bonanza* was in color. So was the sit-com *Hazel*. By the end of the decade, however, most shows would be in color.

There were only a few channels to choose from back then, and getting a good picture was always a challenge. In Chicago, there were the local affiliates of the three major networks – ABC, CBS and NBC – plus two local stations: WGN, an independent station, and our local PBS station. So that's five stations, total.

Hear that, kids? We had *five* TV stations. And none of us watched PBS.

In terms of channel numbers, in Chicago, the networks were 2, 5 and 7. WGN was channel 9 and the PBS station was channel 11.

Your reception came via an antenna that sat atop the TV or a larger antenna on your roof to which the TV was connected. You generally got better reception with the outside antenna. You'd better, as you had no control over that short of your dad climbing onto the roof to fuck with it.

Inside antennae were sometimes called "rabbit ears" because of how they looked when you pulled them out to lengthen them in opposite directions to try to get a better picture. You'd end up positioning them every possible way in this endless quest for a clear picture. (Do TVs still have "horizontal hold?") I usually got the best picture when I held the antenna. As soon as I'd let go the picture got fuzzy again.

If you're a Boomer, you are more than a little familiar with this constantly frustrating exercise, I'm sure. But it leads me to another development that came along in the 1960s that added to the frustration: UHF.

Now they were adding several, higher-number channels to the roster of five existing channels. In Chicago, the new channels were 26, 32 and 44. They were called UHF channels. The old channels were VHF. The UHF channels required a different type of antenna. Now you needed two antennae. And if you thought it was hard to get a good picture on your VHF channels …

Fortunately, at least at first, there wasn't really anything you wanted to watch on the UHF channels. Then the Chicago

White Sox, my favorite baseball team, decided to take their games off VHF station WGN and put them on UHF channel 32. I'd spend half the game up at the TV playing with or holding the UHF antenna. Sometimes I'd intersect the VHF and UHF antennae so they'd be touching each other, thinking that would help. It rarely did.

Channels 26 and 44 were basically throw-away channels. One of them may have been Spanish-speaking, I don't recall. But they weren't mainstream channels.

Channel 32 eventually became the local Fox channel many years later when Fox became a fourth major network. By then, cable TV was beginning to eliminate the headaches of trying to get a good picture via antennae.

To me, that was the greatest benefit of cable TV when it became available in the 1970s. It wasn't all the extra channels or commercial-free movies. It was that you got a perfect picture every time. No longer having to fuck with the damn antennae was truly a blessing for couch potatoes everywhere.

Fields of Dreams

When we moved to the new house, for the first time in my life, I had friends. I learned to ride a two-wheeler and to play sports, which I never did when we lived in the old house. I was terrible at sports at first. I had no brothers and my dad was older than most of my friends' dads, plus he was overweight and not very athletic.

Over time I got much better, as that was all we did was play sports – baseball, football, basketball and hockey. When we were growing up, girls didn't play organized sports. At no point in my childhood did I ever play sports with girls. They weren't allowed in Little League, Pop Warner or any of the other sports leagues I played in. Today, of course, girls can play organized sports, which is as it should be. They just couldn't when I was growing up.

We also didn't play soccer, which has become the most popular organized sport in most communities today. I get it. A lot of kids can run around at the same time and get exercise. It's a simple game in terms of its object. It's outside. It's collective. There is not a lot of individual pressure. Plus, you get healthy snacks at halftime, constant access to water bottles and parents can kibbitz in the stands and get to know each other.

Are you puking yet? Guys who grew up in the '60s, are you gagging? I am just writing this. It's a different world today. More about this in a moment.

Whenever it was nice outside, my mother was all over my ass to "go play outside with all the other kids." She always made it sound like all the kids in the world were part of a big group that was always hanging out together without me. I got the feeling she may not have had a lot of friends growing up and was paranoid that would be me.

With or without my mom's coaxing, I played baseball with my friends virtually every day during the summer, from morning till night. All we needed was four guys to play underhand slow-pitch softball at the park a half-block from my house. We'd close right field, since none of us swung lefty, leaving a pitcher and fielder on each team. If you pulled it too far left, however, that was the street. We're not talking a full-size field here. We're talking a manhole cover for home plate with an improvised field around it.

We ran to first base. It was "pitcher's hands out." If you hit a grounder, as long as the fielder got it to the pitcher before you reached first, you were out. Of course, the arguments were unavoidable. That's how most games ended – with an argument that often resulted in a fight. That or someone's mom showing up telling one of us we had to go home.

We also played what we called "fastball." That's where you draw a chalk square on a brick wall as the strike zone and use a rubber ball. Again, there was a pitcher and a fielder on each team. It was tough to hit. The rubber ball was small and the pitcher was throwing it as hard as he could. When we got older, one of my friends began throwing a curve. These were not high scoring games.

We played "pinners," where the "batter" would one-bounce a rubber ball off a wall and there were boundaries signifying what was a single, double, triple or home run. You could play this with just two people. You also needed just two people to play whiffle ball. You could play this in the front yard because the lightweight ball couldn't do much damage or travel very far – although it constantly got caught in the gutter.

We would play these and other variations of baseball until it was too dark to see, and even then we might attempt to play under the street lights, again until someone's parents made them come in.

For football, like baseball, we found ways to play with as few as four guys, two on a team. On offense, you had a quarterback and receiver. On defense, you had a rusher and a pass defender. The rusher had to count to five ("One one-thousand, two one-thousand," etc.) before he could rush the quarterback. We usually played two-hand touch, although sometimes we played tackle – with no pads or equipment, of course.

Hockey was more often street hockey than ice hockey because ice was not as readily available as the street or a playground. But hockey was big in Chicago in the 1960s. There were only six teams in the NHL at that time and the Chicago Blackhawks were one of them. I played one year in an ice hockey league but I wasn't that good, mostly because I wasn't a great skater.

I played one year of Pop Warner football as well. We played a four-game schedule with full equipment, plays – the real thing. Unfortunately, I didn't get to play any of the "fun" positions – quarterback, running back, receiver, etc. I got stuck playing offensive line, not because I was big but because that's where you got put if you didn't stand out at a skill position.

Today, of course, I imagine they make the coaches play everyone at every position the same amount of plays regardless of ability. That's if today's parents even let their kids play football.

But baseball was always my favorite sport and the one at which I was the best. I played Little League baseball from the earliest age divisions all the way through high school. I rode my bike to practices and games and never missed a contest.

Unlike today, there was no "T-Ball" where you hit the ball off a tee. From the very start, in what they called the "Farm League" (age 6), you hit live pitching. After Farm, there was the Minor League (age 7-9), the Majors (10-12), Senior League (13-15) and Big Boy League (16-18). I played in them all. Your first year in each age group, you'd experience what it was like to be one of the worst guys on the team, but by your third year, you'd feel what it was like to be one of the best.

I had the misfortune of coaching my son in Little League in the 1990s. It's a completely different world out there now.

When I played, if you sucked, you played the minimum three innings that was required, that's all. You batted ninth and they usually stuck you in right field. Today, every kid has to play the same number of innings at every position.

When I played, if I fucked up, the coach told me to get my head out of my ass. Today, it's all positive reinforcement.

"Good try, Billy," when he lets a ball go through his legs.

When I played, only the league champion and runner-up got trophies, and the first-place trophy was much larger than the second-place trophy. Today, every player on every team gets a trophy.

As long as the kids still have fun today, I guess it doesn't matter. But I think it helps you grow up and cope with the realities of life if you're not so babied. It is possible to play to win without disrespecting your opponent. It is possible to lose without it permanently affecting your self-esteem. Experiencing failure is one of the great learning experiences in life. If you are not good enough, work harder to improve. What's wrong with learning to accept disappointment? Today the games seem more like glorified practices.

Am I sounding old or what? Ah, those were the days…

November 22, 1963

If you're a Boomer, you know what happened on this date. You remember where you were and what you were doing. Perhaps no event in our collective lives has had as great an impact.

I was exactly one month shy of turning eight years old. I was in second grade. It was a Friday. I was re-entering the school building with the rest of my class after lunch recess.

"Kennedy just got shot three times in the head," said a fellow second-grader whose class was exiting the building for their recess.

I will never forget that moment. For perhaps the first time in my young life, my heart jumped into my throat. I couldn't believe it.

When we got back to our classroom, the teacher confirmed that President John F. Kennedy had been "assassinated." It was the first time I ever heard that word.

We were told there would be no school on Monday. Of course I was happy about that. Then we were sent home early.

I went with my mom to pick up my sisters at their high school. It was late in the day; cold, gray and raining. I thought it was raining because the president was dead.

Two days later – on Sunday morning, November 24, 1963 – I was at a book fair at my synagogue when word spread that JFK's assassin, Lee Harvey Oswald, had been shot. I was too young to appreciate the implications of the president's killer himself being assassinated. I was too naïve to understand the possibility of Cuban involvement, organized crime, the CIA, Russia or others that could have been linked.

But this was big, just the drama of it. The whole assassination and its aftermath consumed us then and fascinated us for decades to come.

As a seven-year-old, my take on the assassination was simply that this crazy guy – this "assassin" as he was being called – shot the president to be famous or just because he was totally nuts or a criminal, a real "bad guy." And this other guy, Jack Ruby, was trying to be a hero by killing the guy who killed the president.

Of course, I was seven. There are adults that believe this today. Later in life, I became a student of the assassination. I took a college course on it and have read most of the books on it. It is obvious to me that the kill shot came from the front, from the direction of the grassy knoll. It is amazing how many of us bought into the story that it just looks like it came from the front but it really came from the back and hit a nerve that caused the head to snap back as if it came from the front. This is but one of many myths about the assassination.

Today we have a pretty good idea who was behind it, why it was done, how it was done and why the government felt compelled not to pursue the truth. I will let you do the research, as I can't do this subject justice here. Let's just say Oswald may not have even had anything to do with it other than as a pawn in a much more elaborate plan.

But at the time, I didn't question any of this. I was in second grade. Lee Harvey Oswald was an *assassin*. If at that time in my life I were to look up "assassin" in the dictionary, I would have expected to see Oswald's picture.

The JFK assassination was the first big news event I actually remember. To that point in my life, I lived in my own little world, as if life outside didn't exist. The year before the assassination, the world was on the brink of possible annihilation during the Cuban Missile Crisis. I have no recollection of that event.

Life was never the same in the country after JFK was assassinated. It was as if all the promise and hope for the future was gone.

We never took to LBJ – Lyndon Baines Johnson – the vice president under Kennedy who took over the presidency when JFK was killed. Even after his landslide victory over Barry Goldwater in the 1964 election and a progressive social agenda, Johnson came to be associated primarily with escalation of the Vietnam War. He also was not young and handsome like JFK, nor as dynamic a speaker, and was saddled with the perception that he was only president because JFK got killed.

All of this I remember first-hand. I remember nothing of importance before JFK.

For me and many of us Boomers, the JFK assassination signaled an end to our innocence. The rest of the '60s would be filled with turmoil. But first, four lads from Liverpool came to the U.S. and captured the soul of our generation.

Beatlemania

The JFK assassination had brought the whole country down. It's ironic that the Smiley Face was invented that year because we needed it. We needed something to renew the vigor we were feeling before 11/22/63.

My sisters were teenagers entering 1964. I'd just turned eight. I'd grown up hearing Elvis, Ricky Nelson, Connie Francis, Roy Orbison, The Shirelles, Chubby Checker, Fats Domino, Chuck Berry and all the other popular artists of the late '50s and early '60s because my sisters played their records constantly. But to me it was just noise being played too loud that often kept me awake when I was trying to sleep.

This all changed when the Beatles made their first U.S. appearance on the *Ed Sullivan* show the night of Sunday, February 9, 1964. It was 11 weeks since the JFK assassination. More than 70 million people – about 40 percent of the U.S. population at the time – would watch the broadcast. For those of us too young to appreciate Elvis in the '50s, *this* was the birth of rock & roll.

My sisters shared their excitement over the Beatles' upcoming appearance on the Sullivan show as if it were to be some magical event. My parents, avid viewers of Ed Sullivan, would be watching as well. The whole country was abuzz about this group, the Beatles. Even though I wasn't at all familiar with their music, now I was excited just to see what everyone else was so excited about.

When you're eight, you're very impressionable and prone to exaggeration. You build things up in your mind to almost mythical proportions. By the time of the Sullivan show, the Beatles seemed larger than life to me. The funny thing is, they remained larger-than-life, mythical figures through the rest of the decade. They stopped performing live in 1966, adding to their enigma.

When Sullivan announced, "Ladies and Gentlemen, here they are, from Liverpool, England … the Beatles!" the screaming girls and frenzied atmosphere confirmed that I was watching something special. But it was more than that. It was transfor-mational. For the first time in my life, I really got into rock music – the first time I'd gotten into any kind of music. Even more, I felt the *vibe*. You know, the *feeling* you can get from a song, the beat, the emotion. This was all new.

From then on, I was a Beatlemaniac. I started playing my sis-ters' Beatle records. When they moved out of the house, I began buying my own. I got virtually every Beatles single and album as soon as it came out.

For you youngsters out there, a "single" or "45" was a small vinyl disk with two songs on it, one on each side. The "A" side usually had the "hit" song and the "B" side just some random song. But the Beatles were so popular, even the "B" side songs became hits. For example, one single I had contained "I Want to Hold Your Hand" on one side and "I Saw Her Standing There" on the other side.

Singles were called 45s because they rotated at 45 revolutions per minute on the turntable. Albums rotated at 33-1/3 revolutions per minute and were larger, often containing a dozen or more songs.

The Beatles were followed by other rock bands from England, leading some in music circles to call it the "British Invasion." These included the Rolling Stones, the Who, Herman's Hermits, the Hollies and many others.

One of the early British groups to follow the Beatles was the Dave Clark Five. A popular question among my fellow eight-year-olds then was "Who do you like better, the Beatles or the Dave Clark Five?" Everyone knew the Beatles; not many had heard of the Dave Clark Five. Thus, it was cooler to answer that you liked the Dave Clark Five. But if you were being honest, you said you liked the Beatles.

Within a year, there'd be no comparison. At one point during 1964, Beatles songs occupied the top five positions in Billboard's Top 40 Singles in America. They had 13 singles among the top 100. Despite the subsequent emergence of other iconic groups as the Animals, the Byrds, the Turtles, Simon and Garfunkel, the Association and many others – all of whom I liked and bought their albums – no group before or since has had close to the impact of the Beatles.

My grade school cafeteria and day camp bus were replete with Beatles lunch boxes. Beatles posters, board games and other forms of Beatles paraphernalia were in abundance. They even had Beatles trading cards. They were just like baseball cards but they featured the four Beatles.

Beatle haircuts led to the longer hair on boys and young men through the '70s. They made two full-length movies – *A Hard Day's Night* and *Help* – which paved the way for the music videos on which the MTV generation was built.

Whole books have been written and studies conducted on the Beatles' cultural influence on our generation and the world. Anyone out there who lived during Beatlemania and was not influenced in some way was either very sheltered or emotionally numb. They brought first an innocent vitality. Then, they became a force of cultural change – in music, hair styles, fashion, drugs – for our generation. When I think of growing up in the '60s, the Beatles will always be top-of-mind.

And in the end, the love you take is equal to the love you make.

Forty-five years later, the last words written by Lennon and McCartney still ring true.

Evolutionary Wonders

I n 1964, the U.S. Surgeon General reported that cigarette smoking "may lead to" lung cancer. It seems naïve now but this was the first official proclamation that something it seemed almost everyone did could kill you.

Soon there were commercials on television designed to frighten people into not smoking. Even as an eight-year-old who didn't smoke I found them scary.

One of these commercials featured actor William Talman, who played District Attorney Hamilton Burger on the old *Perry Mason* show. Perry Mason was a criminal defense lawyer who won every case. His clients all turned out to be innocent. Of course, this meant District Attorney Burger lost every case.

I used to watch *Perry Mason*. I knew Hamilton Burger. I didn't know William Talman until he began appearing in anti-smoking commercials telling us he was dying of lung cancer and urging us not to smoke. "Don't be a loser," he said.

He died soon afterward. But they continued to run the commercials. That was creepy.

Of course, my dad smoked like a chimney. My mom smoked too, as did all of their friends. They smoked in the house. They smoked in restaurants. They smoked in cars. They smoked in stadiums and arenas. They smoked on airplanes.

Okay, you get it. Now all the sudden, everyone was being told that smoking is bad for you. I'd never thought about it until then.

I remember car trips with my parents to Wisconsin and Minnesota and they would smoke the whole way, often with the windows rolled up. The thought of second-hand smoke being unhealthy to other passengers was never considered.

And, while we're on the subject, that car trip was undoubtedly taken without seat belts. I don't think the car even had them.

Kids, hold onto your hats, but our parents also sent us out trick-or-treating on Halloween at night by ourselves and we knocked on every door. We even ate the popcorn balls, cookies, cupcakes and other homemade items that would get parents charged with child endangerment if they let their kids eat them today.

We were more casual about most things back then. We ate Twinkies. We ate Wonder Bread. Years later, when I had kids of my own, my wife wouldn't let them eat that stuff. But I was allowed to eat it as a kid and somehow I am still here to tell about it. I eat much healthier today, of course. But back then we didn't obsess about food, good or bad, like people do today.

Our parents hired babysitters from the want ads with no background checks. I've mentioned how I had toys at age five that shot projectiles at my face. We had gym teachers and coaches that verbally and physically abused us without ramifications. Our parents disciplined us with belts on bare bottoms for minor transgressions, often out of anger and frustration, which at the time was called parenting.

Hey, I'm not condoning these practices. We know better now. I'm simply asking you – those who believe one whiff of second-hand smoke will give you cancer, or you'll surely have an accident if you don't wear your seat belt, or who won't let their kids play outside, or who analyze their food intake as if they're managing a fool-proof formula for a longer life – How the fuck did we, the Boomers, survive all this? How am I alive today to talk of such self-inflicted mayhem?

Life's a crap-shoot, kids. But I will say this. It shows what a waste it can be to sweat the small stuff. Each of us is alive on this earth such a short time. Mankind itself is still in its infancy. Think how different the world was just 100 years ago. No one in 1915 could have imagined the world we live in today. Now think how different the world will be 100 years from now. The only thing we can be sure of is that most of us probably won't be here; certainly not us Boomers.

Anyone else want a Twinkie?

Civil Rights, Civil Unrest

I was not very politically aware growing up, but by the mid-1960s it was hard not to feel a rumbling under the foundation of our society. The Beatles provided a fun entertainment respite, but otherwise the world seemed a more hostile, volatile place. Or maybe I was just growing up and beginning to notice it wasn't all *Captain Kangaroo* and *Leave it to Beaver*.

Lyndon Johnson was elected president by a landslide over Barry Goldwater in the 1964 presidential election. Most people I knew, including my family, were for Johnson. Of course, we were Jewish and lived in a Jewish area, and most Jews voted Democratic.

LBJ did a lot of good things. He pushed forth a liberal domestic agenda, including the creation of national health insurance for the elderly, otherwise known as Medicare. (Why we can't just extend Medicare to everyone and have a simple national health insurance system like the rest of the world continues to boggle my mind, but that's not for this chapter.)

He signed the Civil Rights Act of 1964, making it illegal to discriminate on the basis of race, religion, sex, national origin or skin color. It also made segregation in schools and public places illegal. All of this should have been a good thing. Yet, when I think of the '60s, all I picture are riots, protests and demonstrations. Obviously, signing something into law doesn't change people's belief systems overnight. Hell, we're still dealing with these issues today.

We really haven't made a lot of progress in race relations in the last 50 years. That's how long ago the Watts riots broke out in Los Angeles. Neighborhood residents were angered by a white policeman's arrest of a black man for DUI. Five days later, 34 people were dead, more than 1,000 injured and 800 buildings burned to the ground or damaged by looters.

Also in 1964, the Warren Report – that great work of fiction on the JFK assassination – was rushed to press with the goal of calming the nation (versus seeking the truth). It was less than a year after the murder in Dallas. That certainly did nothing to reinforce trust in our government institutions.

The Boston Strangler was killing women daily, it seemed. China exploded its first nuclear bomb. Yes, the world suddenly seemed a very hostile place.

The worst, of course, was the Vietnam War. We were just getting into it in the early '60s, but by 1965, there were as many as a half-million U.S. troops fighting in this obscure Southeast Asian country.

Being barely 10 years old at the time, I was still way more engrossed in my baseball cards than by the pictures of body bags increasingly shown on the evening news. But it didn't take too long to pick up on what was going on.

Why the hell are we fighting this war on the other side of the globe? If we really want to win, why not just drop a nuke on

North Vietnam? Oh, they have Russia and China on their side? WHY CAN'T WE ALL JUST GET ALONG?

These were the ruminations of a 10-year-old but in retrospect they weren't that far off. The frustration I remember feeling was that if we can't really "play to win" without provoking World War III, what were we doing then? In the meantime, young men from our country are being forced to go fight in this quagmire whether they believe in the cause or not and are coming home dead.

Again, not much has changed in 50 years, except this was not just our volunteer armed forces being deployed to some distant, dangerous, previously unknown place. These were not people who had decided on their own to join the military because they wanted to serve their country or take advantage of the GI Bill. These were teenagers plucked at random because their draft number came up and they were therefore obligated to put their lives on the line.

I was a little too young to join the anti-war protests that began proliferating throughout the country. Along with the civil rights demonstrations, everyone seemed to be mad at somebody. Young as I was, though, I got it. I had an opinion. I couldn't understand how North Vietnam overtaking South Vietnam would affect us. You'd think the threat of nuclear holocaust would trump the so-called "domino theory." It just seemed like we were fighting someone else's war.

Of course, we still do this. I've been told that's the price you pay for being the world's great superpower. "Would you rather not be?" my hawkish friends ask as if the answer is obvious.

Now, as then, I'm not so sure. It seems more macho than thoughtful. It gives people visceral pleasure. Having the military might to be the world's police force (or bully, depending who you talk to) makes some Americans proud. I'd prefer a world where the concept of deliberately causing as much destruction and killing as many people as possible to solve differences between countries or religious factions is so unthinkable you don't need the strongest country to police it.

Obviously, we have a ways to go in our evolution before this happens. I certainly won't live to see it. But I'd like to think we'll get there someday – if we don't destroy ourselves first.

Frontiers of Adolescence

As the '60s rolled on, I was leaving the innocence of childhood for the frontiers of adolescence. I suddenly saw and understood more of the world around me ... and it wasn't all good. Still, there was a carry-over from the '50s and early '60s in terms of new inventions, technologies and cultural icons to be enjoyed.

Touch-tone phones were the new big thing. They replaced rotary, or dial, phones. They were trimmer and more colorful, and the buttons and sounds made them seem so modern if not futuristic. (But they were still landlines, kids.)

Zip codes were implemented. I remember people wondering how they'd remember all those numbers.

Pull-tabs were put on pop cans. (Being from Chicago, I call carbonated beverages "pop," not "soda.") You pulled them off and had to throw them away. It would be a few years before they came up with the kind they have today that don't come off. But it sure beat having to use a can opener.

The biggest toy craze was the Super Ball. Holy shit! Sorry, but man!

Okay, for the record, we're talking about a small, very hard rubber ball that could bounce hundreds of times farther and faster (it seemed) than any ball any of us had ever seen or played with. And it could be downright dangerous!

I have memories of playing pinners between the side of my house and the wall of our detached garage with a Super Ball. Both walls were brick. In between was a small cement patio that couldn't have been more than 20 feet across, maybe less. If you've ever played pinners, think about this for a moment. If you haven't, sorry I made you read this paragraph.

Some of my favorite movies of all time came out in 1967. These included *Bonnie and Clyde*, *Cool Hand Luke*, *The Graduate* and *Guess Who's Coming to Dinner*.

Guess Who's Coming to Dinner was controversial at the time because it dealt with interracial marriage, which was actually illegal in some states. Coincidentally or not, that same year the U.S. Supreme Court declared interracial marriage constitutional, and thus, could no longer be deemed a crime.

I was too young to see *The Graduate* when it first came out. I think it may even have been rated X, although I can't imagine why. I saw it a couple years later, however, when it was re-released in the theaters (there was still no cable or pay-per-view, kids) and it ended up actually having some influence in my life.

I identified with Dustin Hoffman's character. It taught me (falsely) that you can win unrequited love through drastic measures. It influenced my decision to apply to Berkeley for college. For whatever reason, it is one of just a handful of movies I can still enjoy watching over and over no matter how many times I've seen it.

Despite no cable, television really started coming into its own in 1967. For the first time, the majority of shows were in color and reception seemed better. I still liked the sit-coms: *The Beverley Hillbillies, Lucy, Bewitched, I Dream of Jeanie,* and a new show that had an impact on me, *The Monkees.*

I would turn 12 at the end of 1967. I was in the latter part of grade school. Being popular and fitting in was so important, and also so dependent, in my mind, on personal appearance. The Monkees, being an American rock band (albeit one created specifically for this show), kind of brought the Beatles home to kids my age. In other words, we were a little too young to try to imitate the Beatles. That was for my sisters' age group – the Early Boomers. For the kids at my school, the Monkees became the role models.

Pokka-dot, paisley and flowered button-down shirts I could do. I could wear the tight pants with the wide belt. What I couldn't do was the popular hair style of the time: the long, straight hair with bangs that you could flip back with a snap of your neck. I had curly hair; Jew hair, if you will. It was the bane of my adolescent existence. It was the main cause of my insecurity. I honestly felt if I had straight hair I would be *much* more popular.

So, one day, my sisters offered to straighten my hair. I think I was in sixth grade. They used a product called "Curl Free." It worked fantastic. My hair was exactly the way I'd always wanted it. I could flip it back and everything. I couldn't wait to go to school the next day.

The next day was one of the worst of my life. I was ridiculed mercilessly. I couldn't wait for my natural hair to grow out or the Curl Free to wear off, whatever it took to look like myself again. Never again was I tempted to straighten my hair.

We liked the Monkees' music too, but we were teeny-boppers. My sisters and the rest of the Early Boomers were starting to groove to bands like Cream, The Doors, The Grateful Dead, Jimi Hendrix, Janis Joplin and Jefferson Airplane.

All in all, the second half of the '60s was shaping up to be an adolescent nightmare. The personal changes and insecurities would be accompanied by a drastically changing domestic climate. Long hair, miniskirts, the anti-war movement, the women's movement, the civil rights movement, sex and drugs and rock & roll were creating huge divisions among people.

The biggest, of course, was the so-called "generation gap." I'm sure there is a gap between all generations – I know there is between me and my kids – but this one in the '60s was on steroids. All of the sudden, our generation seemed in color while our folks were still in black-and-white (that TV metaphor again).

I probably shouldn't generalize. Not everyone "turned on and dropped out." Some young people still thought like their parents about the war, long hair or civil rights, while some parents were more progressive in their thinking than others. But for the most part, young people were incensed about their peers getting killed in Vietnam while defending someone else's crappy little country, while the older generation felt it unpatriotic to question our role in the war.

Our generation also began to question the country's Victorian-like stuffiness when it came to using more mind-expanding drugs than alcohol, and a loosening of sexual morals. For some parents, these kinds of behaviors were beyond sacrilegious. They were nothing short of the beginning of the end of civilization.

Peace, Love and Hepatitis

In 1967, young people throughout the country flocked to San Francisco for what was dubbed "the summer of love." Members of this so-called "counter-culture" rejected the Cold War-era morals and values of the "establishment" (loosely defined as people over 30). They sought greater enhancement, fulfillment and meaning from life through music, drugs, communal living, free sex and other pleasurable, creative and/or mind-expanding outlets. They decried money and consumerism, didn't trust the government, and were strongly opposed to the Vietnam War. They were known as "hippies" or sometimes "flower children."

I say "they" because I wasn't one of them ... yet. I was still too young. I wouldn't turn 12 till the end of the year. My social consciousness meter was still in the very low range. If you ask me what I remember most about the summer of 1967, it was the Chicago White Sox blowing the American League pennant the final weekend of the season when they had been tied for first with three other teams (the Detroit Tigers, Minnesota Twins and Boston Red Sox) when the weekend began. The Red Sox won it and lost the World Series in seven games to the St. Louis Cardinals. I even remember Bob Gibson dominating

Boston ace Jim Lonborg in Game 7. Of course, Lonborg was pitching on just two days' rest.

So that's where my head was at. My sister Michele got married in January 1967. She was 21. My other sister, Lynne, turned 19 that summer and made the pilgrimage to the West Coast. She ended up moving there and becoming an official hippie. She lived with several other hippies in one of those old Victorian-style houses that characterized San Francisco's Haight-Ashbury district. The Jefferson Airplane were among their neighbors.

Lynne soon fell in love with another hippie, Brian, and they planned to get married. I flew with my parents to California for the wedding. I'd never been to California. In fact, it was the first time I flew on an airplane. All of my previous vacations had been by car except for one, when we took a train to Minnesota.

Lynne's housemates were so cool to a wide-eyed 11-year-old, and I idolized Brian. I'd never had a brother. I liked Michele's husband too.

Brian had long, shaggy brown hair, was tall and thin and wore very cool clothes. He looked like a cross between Peter Noone, lead singer of Herman's Hermits, and Peter Fonda in the movie *Easy Rider*. He also talked with that California accent, which I also found very cool.

My first day there, I got to spend a whole afternoon with Brian, just me and him, driving around San Francisco. He drove a small car with a stick shift and picked up every hitchhiker we came across. I'd never picked up hitchhikers before.

I mean, I didn't drive, but my parents never picked up hitch-hikers. I was a little nervous at first. But most of the people we picked up were also young people just going about their afternoon.

Lynne's housemates included another couple, Alan and Linda, both of whom had long, straight hair down their backs; Linda's was blonde, Alan's dark brown. On future visits, I would learn that Alan was gay, but on this visit, he and Linda were together, and I believe even married.

Another member of the household was Tim, who they called Mother. He was openly gay, yet at the time I didn't think so because that's how sheltered and naïve I was. He looked like a cross between Paul McCartney and pop star Bobby Sherman. They called him Mother because that's sort of the role he played in the house. If someone couldn't find their socks, he'd know where they were.

Then there was Stuart. With his long, scraggly light hair and beard, he looked like a young Santa Claus. He was very laid back. One night we had dinner with Lynne and her friends at their house. They had made some salad dressing out of mayonnaise and ketchup. Stuart came in, sat down at the table, and drawled, "Hey man, this is the best fucking Russian dressing ever, man."

Mother (Tim, not my mother) started laughing. "It's just mayonnaise and ketchup," he said.

"Well," Stuart said, "It's still the best fucking Russian dressing I've ever had."

I loved these people.

The visit also marked the first time I'd seen marijuana. My parents let me stay at Lynne's one night while they went back to the hotel. There must have been at least a dozen people sitting in a circle on the floor in the living room. It was dark, music playing. When the joint came to me, I looked at Lynne, not knowing what to do. She told me if I didn't want any to just pass it on, which I did.

I also saw my first rock concert: Taj Mahal and Boz Scaggs at the Fillmore. Actually, my dad had taken me to see Louis Armstrong in Chicago about a year before, but that was all old people. This was a rock concert with a bunch of hippies at the Fillmore in San Francisco during the summer of love! Many more joints were passed my way during the concert but I still didn't indulge. Again, I was only 11. I didn't start smoking pot till I was 15.

Lynne and Brian were married in a civil ceremony at city hall. My parents and I and all their hippie friends were there. I remember sitting in the gallery of the courtroom waiting for a traffic case involving a VW bus to conclude before the judge could marry them. That night, my parents hosted a dinner for everyone at a nice seafood restaurant on Fisherman's Wharf.

Following the trip, I remember Lynne and Brian getting very sick with hepatitis. I didn't know what hepatitis was. I certainly didn't know that it was being contracted by an increasing number of drug users sharing needles to inject heroin and other hard drugs. I don't think my parents knew either. Maybe they did.

Lynne and Brian got better, but it's like the lid on Pandora's Box of illegal drugs had been lifted. Marijuana is one thing;

heroin and psychedelics are another. The hippie era ushered in experimentation with all kinds of mind-altering substances in an attempt to expand one's consciousness in search of a utopian high.

Some people could handle it. Others fell into the abyss of drug addiction. My sister – both of my sisters, actually – were in the latter category. Fortunately, they both survived and have now been sober for more than 30 years. Others went the way of Janis Joplin, Jimi Hendrix and Jim Morrison.

It was a transformational summer, that summer of 1967, even for an 11-year-old who would not smoke his first joint for several more years. I had been exposed to a culture I found intriguing, magical, risky, edgy, mysterious and fun all at the same time. Let's just say Skokie suddenly seemed a most shallow and boring place. I couldn't wait to go back to visit Lynne and her friends myself, without my parents, which I would do annually for more than a decade.

That little kid who played with baseball cards and marbles on the floor was gone.

The Convention

The year 1968 was a presidential election year. The Democratic National Convention would be held in Chicago.

The war in Vietnam was tearing the country apart. In January, the Tet offensive marked the most aggressive strike against U.S. and South Vietnamese troops since the war began. It turned even more Americans against the war. It was becoming increasingly apparent that this damn war was unwinnable. In the meantime, the number of U.S. troops in South Vietnam now exceeded 500,000.

We were not just against the war, but also the draft. It seemed worse than forced servitude. At least with that you had a reasonable chance of surviving. With the way this war was going (and growing), getting drafted seemed like a death sentence. Getting drafted to fight in a war you didn't believe in seemed like being sentenced to death for a crime you didn't commit. American soldiers being sent to Vietnam were younger than those that served in World War II – average age 19 versus 26 – making this particularly oppressive to our generation.

Then the shit really began to hit the fan. In March, while announcing the deployment of 13,500 additional troops to

Vietnam, President Johnson also said that he "would not seek, nor will I accept" the Democratic nomination for president in the 1968 election. The pressure of the war was too much for him. He didn't say that, but that was the main reason he chose not to run. Vice President Hubert Humphrey became the choice of the Democratic establishment.

Four days later, on April 4, civil rights leader Martin Luther King was shot and killed as he stood on a motel balcony in Memphis. The black community in more than 100 U.S. cities vented their rage by breaking windows, turning over cars, burning buildings and looting businesses. So now, in addition to all the anti-war protests, there were race riots going on all over the country.

In May, more than 2,000 American soldiers died in Vietnam. It was the worst monthly toll to date. Anti-war candidates like senators Eugene McCarthy and Bobby Kennedy, JFK's brother, had entered the presidential fray as non-establishment options to Hubert Humphrey, giving hope to those who desperately wanted the war to end. Bobby Kennedy, like his brother, was particularly popular with the younger generation, winning primaries and gaining delegates to provide a challenge to Humphrey.

Then, on June 5, two months after the assassination of Martin Luther King, Bobby Kennedy was shot and killed in the kitchen of a hotel ballroom in Los Angeles after winning the California primary. "Now it's on to Chicago and let's win there," were his last words.

I mean, what next? That's what everyone was thinking. And the year wasn't even half over.

While RFK had been no shoe-in to wrest the nomination from Humphrey, his assassination, like the JFK assassination, was a huge blow to many of us Boomers. I sometimes think about what this country would be like had neither Kennedy been killed. JFK probably would have been president through 1968. From what I've read, he was not a hawk when it came to Vietnam, and was smart and decisive enough to have found a better solution than escalating the war as LBJ did.

It's possible that Bobby would have succeeded JFK and held the presidency from 1968-1976. Then it might have been Ted's turn (if we also assume Chappaquiddick would not have happened). We might have had Kennedys in the White House for 24 years!

Of course it's all conjecture, but a country that was growing more liberal and progressive at the onset of the '60s meshed with the smart and youthful Kennedys. There was an allure that was palpable. It is why those assassinations hurt us so deeply.

We can only look back ruefully at what might have been. The agenda for the country would have been far different than the morass it devolved into under Nixon, Ford, Carter, Reagan and the Bushes. Bill Clinton – the first Baby Boomer elected president – has had the most successful presidency in my lifetime so far, and by a wide margin.

But back to the convention. RFK's assassination set up a free-for-all among Democrats for someone else to challenge Humphrey for the presidential nomination. There was still McCarthy, who was definitely anti-war but didn't have much charisma. Then, just two weeks before the convention, a candidate by the name of George McGovern emerged. As the August convention approached, this 12-year-old non-voter, for whatever reason, found himself supporting McGovern.

The week of the convention, the city of Chicago was set up like a war zone. Thousands of anti-war protesters from throughout the country descended on the city to participate in organized rallies, marches and demonstrations. Chicago Mayor Richard Daley did not want his city embarrassed. He told police to do whatever it took to maintain order. In addition to 12,000 Chicago police, 15,000 state and federal officers were called in, along with another 15,000 Illinois National Guardsmen and U.S. military troops.

It was into this atmosphere that my friend Craig and I thought it would be fun to crash the convention.

Actually, we just wanted to go downtown and see what was going on. I was not yet allowed to take the "L" – Chicago's subway system that actually runs more above ground than below – into the city. But I'd done it before. We used to go to this novelty store where they sold fake vomit, plastic ice cubes with flies in them, whoopee cushions and other hilarious shit like that.

The great thing about going anywhere with Craig was that he paid for everything. That's because he stole money from his parents.

We used to go to this amusement park by our house called Fun Fair. Before there were giant Six Flaggs amusement parks across the country, there were smaller fun parks in local communities. They were like the traveling carnivals they have today, but they were permanent. Fun Fair had a Wild Mouse (a very tame roller coaster by today's standards), Tilt-a-Whirl and other rides, plus cotton candy and all that. It was close enough to my house to ride my bike there. And, as I said, Craig paid for everything.

The 1968 Democratic National Convention was being held at Chicago's International Amphitheater, about a mile from downtown. The police wouldn't allow demonstrators any-where near the convention site (there were shoot-to-kill orders, I'm not kidding) so most of the marches and demon-strations were in Grant Park downtown, and Lincoln Park, north of the downtown area. (I would do my first illegal drug, a Quaalude, in Lincoln Park a year or two later.)

We took the train to the heart of the Loop, Chicago's main downtown business district. The instant we walked out onto the street from the subway exit, we were bombarded by people handing out buttons, bumper stickers, banners, posters and other campaign crap. Most of it was for Humphrey, McCarthy or McGovern, but I swear I brought home some Nixon stuff too. (Richard Nixon, who lost narrowly to JFK in the 1960 presidential election, was the 1968 Republican nominee.)

When we told the McGovern campaign workers we were for McGovern, they took us up to their headquarters in this big office building and gave us more stuff. They had to know we were too young to vote but maybe they thought it would influence our parents' vote in the next election? McGovern wasn't going to get this nomination. Humphrey had it all but locked up at this point.

Whatever, we were 12 and made it our business to fill several shopping bags worth of stuff to bring home. Just being downtown and "participating" in the national presidential race was exciting. It wasn't until we were on the train home, figuring out what to tell our parents, that we realized we never even checked out any of the marches, demonstrations and other protest activity we'd heard about.

When my parents asked me where I got all the stuff, I told them they were giving it out in downtown Skokie. That sounded reasonable. I don't know if they believed me but at the time they seemed satisfied.

A day or two later, toward the end of convention week, my sisters went downtown to participate in a big anti-war rally. The protesters then planned to march to the Amphitheater where the convention was taking place. That never happened as police began clubbing not just the demonstrators, but journalists, emergency aid workers and even innocent bystanders.

My parents watched in horror as all of this played out on the evening news. Then my mom sent my dad downtown to find my sisters and bring them home.

Think about that for a moment. This was way before cell phones, kids. My folks had no idea where my sisters were. Yet somehow my dad did find them and brought them home. Of course, it was the next day. I believe they all spent the night in the slammer first.

I'm not sure what it all accomplished. Humphrey was nominated. He lost the election to Nixon. The Vietnam War continued. The country was more divided than ever. As we approached the end of the 1960s, a decade that began with such great promise could not end soon enough.

One Small Step

Anyone else need a pick-me-up? We all did. It would come in July 1969 when a human being actually walked on the moon.

In 1961, President Kennedy had promised to put a man on the moon by the end of the decade, and I'll be damned, it actually happened. I was playing baseball in the street when it started to get dark. I remember being anxious to get home to watch the moon walk on TV.

That night, I watched in fascination with my parents as the grainiest black-and-white images I'd ever seen flashed across the screen. This was actually happening on the moon! On the fucking moon!!

NASA subsequently began sending astronauts to the moon on a fairly regular basis. By the 70s, they were driving cars up there and beaming back images in color. Yet, after that first time, nobody seemed interested. Talk about jaded! How can you have a "been there, done that" attitude about going to the moon? And after just one trip! But that's what I remember.

We haven't been to the moon since.

Also in 1969 was the Woodstock music festival in New York State. I wasn't there but I went to plenty of iconic concerts in the 1970s. Eric Clapton, Santana, the Who, Paul McCartney and Wings, Frank Zappa and many others. Also in 1969, the Beatles recorded their final album together, *Abbey Road*. It was not the last album they released, but the last they recorded.

That summer also saw Charles Manson and his hippie worshippers from the Bizarro World kill actress Sharon Tate and several house guests in cold blood. Then they did the same thing to another couple in the same upper-class Hollywood neighborhood the next night. About a week later, I was watching a late-night program on Saturday night called *Playboy After Dark* in which Hugh Hefner hosts a party, presumably at the Playboy mansion, with celebrities among the guests. That night, one of the guests was Sharon Tate. That was eerie.

For me, though, the summer of 1969 was mostly about the '69 Chicago Cubs. I was 13. My parents finally felt I was old enough to take the "L" to Wrigley Field. From our house in Skokie, I would walk two blocks to the bus stop, take the bus to the Skokie Swift (a commuter train), take the Swift to the Howard Street "L" station, and the L train to Addison Street, a block from Wrigley. All that cost 50 cents.

Bleacher seats at Wrigley were $1 and were general admission, so if you got there early enough you could get first row. Seats went on sale at 9 a.m. The Cubs played all day games then. Wrigley Field wouldn't get lights for another 20 years.

I usually went to the games with my friend Larry. Before getting in line at the bleacher window, we'd go across the street to a hamburger stand named Henry's (a local precursor to McDonald's) and each get five hamburgers for $1. The Andy Frain ushers let us bring them into the park. The only things you couldn't bring in were bottles and cans.

So, if you do the math, that's $3 for round-trip transportation, a front-row seat and five burgers. If your parents gave you $5, that left you with $2 more to spend on pop, Frosty Malts and other concessions during the game. Given that each of those items was probably a quarter, you can imagine the damage a 13-year-old could do on a long summer day.

One time we accidentally took the wrong train. We didn't realize it until we saw Wrigley Field come and go through the window. We got off at the next stop and got on a different train. This one also did not stop at Addison. It took us eight trains before one finally did. We took quite a tour of the city that morning, going through some pretty seedy areas – scary stuff for a couple of white kids from Skokie.

Another time, the line at the Addison L stop after the game was so long we decided to walk under the tracks to the next station. Along the way we encountered a bum barbequing what looked like a dog on a stick over an open flame. I have never been able to erase that image from my mind.

It was an exciting season. The Cubs were in first place most of the way. They had four future Hall of Famers on that team: Ernie Banks, Billy Williams, Ron Santo and Ferguson Jenkins. Their manager also was a Hall of Famer: Leo Durocher. Then the New York Mets – who had never had a winning season before in their history – caught fire and the Cubs could not keep up. The so-called "Miracle Mets" won 100 games, eight more than the Cubs, and then proceeded to win the World Series over the heavily favored Baltimore Orioles.

I don't know how many games we went to that year but it was a lot. While we usually sat in the bleachers, Larry's dad bought us box seats for one game that season. He even drove us there in his Cadillac. It was the first time I'd ridden in a Cadillac. It was so smooth, so quiet.

We sat maybe 20 rows behind the first base dugout. The Cubs were playing the Atlanta Braves. Cub pitcher Ken Holtzman threw a no-hitter that day. Late in the game, the Braves' Hank Aaron – another Hall of Famer – hit a towering fly to left that looked like it was headed onto Waveland Avenue. The wind or some supernatural force knocked it down and Billy Williams caught it in the "well" in left field with his back against the vines.

I didn't know it at the time, but my current wife – the love of my life – was also at that game, seated not far in front of me. It would be another 40 years before we would meet.

Busted

For me, the new decade coincided with the start of high school. What a painful time. You're supposed to have fun but your hormones are raging and you are so ill-equipped to handle it. It probably only seemed like I was more insecure than everyone else, but it's a fact that I could never make the first move with a girl. She literally had to tackle me first.

Compounding matters was that the hippies, with all their so-called "free love," had complicated the dating game. Dating in the conventional sense was now passé, like it was no longer cool for a guy to ask a girl "out" on a "date." We weren't exactly sure what we were supposed to do instead, but when you are as insecure as I was, this stuff was paralyzing.

By junior year, I began drinking and smoking pot with my friends. We didn't drink much. Alcohol never seemed to agree with me. But I drank it on occasion and usually ended up acting like a moron and/or throwing up.

Marijuana never affected me like alcohol. I'd been exposed to it for years but always turned it down. Then one day, for no particular reason, I took the joint when it was passed to me and never looked back.

The first few times I smoked, I couldn't tell if it had any effect. Then one day we're in the car (we usually smoked in someone's car) and I started laughing at something uncontrollably. As I'm laughing, I started seeing my surroundings frame-by-frame, like an old silent movie. I was stoned.

Still, smoking pot was mostly just a social thing for me in high school. I never bought any. I never owned any. What we smoked was never mine. I just did it because my friends did it.

One night at the start of my senior year, five of us were heading home after a night of riding around getting high in my friend Stu's car. It was a Thursday night, or technically Friday morning, about 2 a.m. Yes, it was a school night and we were out past curfew, but that was pretty much the norm. My official curfew was midnight but my parents didn't really enforce it.

The last place we'd been was a Dunkin Donuts, where a guy who looked like a zombie from *Night of the Living Dead* – pale, long greasy hair, bloodshot eyes – stumbled in and bellowed, "Hey, did anyone here see The Dead?"

He meant the rock group, The Grateful Dead. This was 1973.

"No," someone shouted back. "Did you?"

"Hell no, man" he said. "I saw the Allman Brothers, man."

As we're driving home, Stu noticed another friend of ours, Steve, behind us. Stu pulled over on a side street and Steve pulled next to him. They had plans the next day or something, so they talked briefly, then Steve drove off. Just as Stu was about to do the same, a Skokie police car came up behind us, bubbles flashing. Suddenly an Officer Schultz was at Stu's window.

"Okay, who's got the grass?" Schultz asked.

Officer Schultz was peering through the rolled-down driver's side window. Next to Stu in the front seat was Paula, a girl who didn't usually hang with us but did on this night. Next to her was my friend Jami. I was in back with my friend Paul.

"Grass?" Stu said in mock disbelief. "What grass? We don't have any grass."

Of course, the car reeked of pot. Schultz asked for everyone's IDs. Then there's a rap on the front passenger side window. Another cop is standing there. Jami rolled down the window.

"What'd you just put under the seat?" the cop asked Jami.

Unbeknownst to me, Paula had a nickel bag of pot in her purse. Certain they would search her purse, she took it out and put it on Jami's lap. Jami, in turn, put it under his seat.

"Nothing officer," Jami said. "I just dropped my comb. It fell out when I was reaching for my wallet."

Later, while reviewing the events of the evening, I thought that was a great answer. I really admired Jami for coming up with something so plausible so fast, in the heat of the moment. It was common to keep a comb in your back pocket back then. At the time, however, I still didn't know about the bag of pot.

"Get out of the car," the officer told Jami.

Then Schultz comes over, looks under the front seat, grabs the bag of pot and waves it in front of Jami's face. That was the first I'd seen of this bag all night.

"Comb, huh!" he yells in Jami's face. "Comb, huh!" He was pissed.

I think Schultz threatened to bust Jami's skull for lying to him. The cops frisked Jami thoroughly, even made him unbuckle his pants and jump up and down.

Jami could be such a jerk. If this weren't so serious I'd say he had it coming. But on this night, we were all in this nightmare together.

The cops made all of us get out of the car and frisked and handcuffed us. For me they used these one-piece handcuffs that got tighter if you put any pressure on them – which happened when they threw me in the back of a squad car.

When we reached the Skokie police station, they took everyone's handcuffs off – except mine. Mine needed a special key.

"Hey Joe," Schultz yelled. "You got the key to these handcuffs?"

"I think we lost it," was the reply.

"Well, I guess we'll have to cut 'em off," Schultz said.

Schultz takes out a knife, looks me in the eye and asks, "Do you bleed easily?"

Taken aback a bit, with my wrists aching from those damn handcuffs, I managed to say, "Yes, I bleed very easily."

"We'll try to be careful then," Schultz said.

He proceeds to cut the one-piece, plastic handcuffs from my wrists as I closed my eyes and gritted my teeth.

Then they started going through our possessions. Among Stu's possessions was what looked like a bullet, but when you pulled it apart it was actually a roach clip. The cops got a big kick out of that.

"Hey Joe," Schultz yelled in what had now become his typical bombastic style. "Do your bullets do this? My bullets don't do this." These guys should play Zanie's.

Then they got serious and tried to get us to tell them where we got the pot. We didn't have any big pot connections. When we wanted pot, we asked people if they knew anyone who might have some. But this pot was Paula's. I didn't even know she had it. None of us had any idea where she got it. As I said, she usually didn't hang with us.

When we went out, we always rolled a few joints beforehand to bring with us. We never brought a bag of loose pot in the car because it would be too hard to get rid of if we got stopped. Joints you could swallow if you had to. The rule of thumb was never to bring more than you could eat.

But we weren't going to pin this on Paula. Telling the cops the pot was hers and the rest of us didn't know anything about it wouldn't have helped us anyway. So we told the cops we bought the bag earlier that evening from a stranger in Gilson Park, a park on Chicago's north shore where we sometimes hung out.

They pressed further, trying to scare us into divulging the source of the nickel bag, which had a street value back then of about $5.

"Did you know this stuff can cause brain damage?" Schultz said. "BRAIN DAMAGE!" he yelled louder.

You'd think these guys just nabbed the heads of some international drug cartel. We're talking $5 worth of pot.

Then it was time for mug shots and fingerprints. For whatever reason, I couldn't get my fingers to relax enough for the fingerprint person to roll my fingers the way they wanted me to. They had to start over several times. They were getting upset. They actually threatened me.

"Okay, we're gonna do this one more time and that's it!" But what did that mean? They didn't tell me what the consequences would be if I fucked up again. Did it mean I wouldn't have to get my fingerprints taken? Or did it mean they would beat me up, put me in jail, or worse?

It didn't matter, as the last go-around was acceptable. Then we were taken back to the room where we were first processed and allowed to call our parents.

Stu went first. "Mom? Let me talk to Dad." Pause. "Mom, just let me talk to Dad." Another pause, then his dad got on the line and Stu told him what happened.

This scenario comically repeated itself for each one of us. Our mothers answered the phone, as they were probably panicking a little as to where we were at three in the morning on a school night (again, there were no cell phones, kids). But we each felt more comfortable telling our dads what happened.

I was the last to call. My mom answered. "Mom, let me talk to Dad," I said.

"Where are you?" she inquired.

"Mom, just let me talk to Dad."

"We've been worried sick. Where are you?"

"Mom, please, would you just let me talk to Dad?"

Everyone else, their mothers turned the phone over to their fathers by the second try. Not me. My mom kept grilling me. She wouldn't put my dad on. It was very embarrassing. I wouldn't tell her anything. Finally, she let me talk to my dad.

We were able to wait in the processing room for our parents to come and pay the $100 bail to get each of us out. They didn't put us in jail cells.

Soon the parents started showing up. My dad walked in with a wad of money in his hand looking to pay someone off. But the cops didn't bite so he had no choice but to just bail me out legally like everyone else.

We were eventually sentenced to 12 months of court supervision. If we didn't get busted again in that period, our records would be expunged.

Toward the end of my senior year, my parents went out of town. I had several parties at the house in which a lot of pot was smoked. Fortunately, there were no issues with police. I cleaned the house thoroughly before my folks got back.

The next day, I'm sitting in the den watching TV when my mom walks in.

"How much pot was smoked here while we were gone?" she demanded.

"None that I know of," I lied.

"Well, then what are *these*?" She was holding a pack of Zig Zag rolling papers that I must have missed during my clean-up. I'll never forget how strange it looked to see my mom holding a pack of rolling papers. "I didn't even know what these were," she said. "I had to ask your father."

Busted again.

Today, America finally seems to be coming to its senses and on the path to legalizing marijuana. But my God; is this taking long or what? And it still may be awhile. As of this writing, only a few states have legalized it for recreational use, and even in those places there are restrictions on how much you can buy. There are no such restrictions for alcohol, cigarettes or even guns.

Then there is this ridiculous interim step in most states of first legalizing marijuana for "medicinal" use. They did that with alcohol too during Prohibition. Hello? Can't we just legalize this stuff, tax and regulate it like alcohol and cigarettes, and move on?

Don't we Baby Boomers deserve at least this much in our lifetimes?

You Capitalist Pig

My number came up in the 300s in the draft lottery my senior year of high school. This would have caused a sigh of relief – the higher the number out of the 366 birthdays to choose from, the less chance of you being drafted – were it not for the fact that by then the government was no longer drafting kids to serve in Vietnam.

We began pulling our troops out in 1973 following a cease-fire agreement with North Vietnam. We had achieved "peace with honor," as President Nixon called it. The last American personnel left Vietnam on April 30, 1975, as the South Vietnam capital of Saigon fell to communist forces and became Ho Chi Minh City. North and South Vietnam were subsequently unified under communist rule as the Socialist Republic of Vietnam.

So, after all that, we lost the war. You can call it "peace with honor" but we lost. We fought to keep North Vietnam from taking over South Vietnam and creating a unified communist government, and we failed. More than 3 million Americans served in the war. Nearly 60,000 were killed, 300,000 were wounded, and more than 1,000 are still missing in action. Did we learn something? I sure hope so. Because if not, I'm not sure what was gained.

In June 1972, as Nixon was running for re-election, five men were arrested for breaking into the offices of the Democratic National Committee at Washington's Watergate hotel and office complex. Nixon won re-election handily over Democrat George McGovern in the fall election. But his involvement in the Watergate break-in and subsequent cover-up cost him the presidency. Facing impeachment and with little public support, he resigned in August 1974, turning over the presidency to Vice President Gerald Ford.

As the Fords were moving their stuff into the President's wing of the White House, I was moving mine into a tiny, un-air conditioned, brick-walled dorm room at the University of Wisconsin-Madison. The communal bathroom was at the end of the hall, across from the elevator.

I knew virtually no one. Most of my friends from high school went to the University of Illinois in Champagne. For in-state residents, it cost about a third of what my dad was paying for me to go to Madison. But he said I could go wherever I wanted and I didn't want to go where all my friends were going. I wanted college to be a new experience. I applied to Champagne. I also applied to Michigan State and Cal State-Berkeley. I got into all of them. I chose Madison.

Berkeley was tempting, especially with my sister and her friends living across the bay in San Francisco. But California just seemed too far away for someone who had never lived away from home. Madison was the Berkeley of the Midwest, a beautiful campus, liberal as they come, yet just a 2-1/2 hour drive from Chicago.

I could have gotten a single room in the dorm, but introvert that I am, I figured it would be immensely easier to make friends and meet people if I had a roommate. On the questionnaire, I had put down that I wanted a smoker even though I didn't smoke cigarettes because I figured someone who smoked cigarettes would be more likely to smoke pot. All my high school friends smoked cigarettes. It didn't bother me. I grew up with it. We all did.

Ironically, the roommate they picked for me had put down on his questionnaire that he wanted a non-smoker because he hated cigarette smoke. The Cosmos must have intervened because the way it turned out, both of us smoked pot and neither of us smoked cigarettes. Go figure. Jeff became and remained my best friend during my four years at Madison.

Jeff was from Appleton, Wisconsin, a typical small Wisconsin town centrally located in the state. For him and his friends and other students from these small Wisconsin towns, the move to Madison was more than just going away to college. Madison was the state capital and Wisconsin's second-largest city, providing a new, exciting urban environment to explore. Being from Chicago, I didn't share this fascination. Madison is a small town compared to Chicago.

For me, it was the liberalism of the campus and the rebellious nature of the students toward the Establishment that provided the biggest change from home. We all shared the long hair and scruffy clothes. We all smoked pot. But Jeff and his friends from Appleton were much more politically aware than I was. They were particularly hostile toward our economic system, i.e., capitalism.

They detested wealth. They reveled in being poor. Large corporations were evil. McDonald's was like Satan. They seemed to reject work itself if it is done solely to make money. Ideally, you should grow your own food and contribute to society and your personal fulfillment through art, writing or other creative endeavors.

We Baby Boomers were born in America's most affluent time. Our parents wanted us to go to college so we could get a good job and make a good living. By the time we were ready for college, however, the landscape had changed. Making money was out of style. "You capitalist pig" they'd call you if you went into some field strictly for the money, thus becoming part of the Establishment.

Wanting to fit in, I bought into this mindset. Hey, I was cool. I was a product of the '60s, man.

Had it not been for this mindset, there is a good chance I would have been an accountant or something like that. Math was always my best subject in school. It seemed a simple thing to learn some formulas and plug in numbers. It was so objective.

If I wanted to be cool, however, I needed to do something else, something more creative. This is what led me to major in journalism and become a writer – peer pressure. How pathetic is that? If the bureaucrats doling out dorm assignments had placed me with a different roommate, I may have majored in finance, become a millionaire and lived in a mansion on the beach. Or my private jet might have malfunctioned and I wouldn't be writing this.

Again, life's a crapshoot, kids.

While most colleges swayed left in the late '60s and early '70s, with anti-war protests and civil rights demonstrations common on all campuses, Madison was considered one of the more radical. When Dow Chemical, maker of napalm, was recruiting on campus in 1967, protesting students took over the Commerce Building (of course) and police had to use tear gas to quell the riot.

In 1970, a group of radicals bombed the Math Research Center – a facility funded by the U.S. Army – killing a physics professor and injuring four others. This, admittedly, was not one of the anti-war movement's finest hours.

Nonetheless, these and other incidents fueled Madison's reputation as a hotbed for political activism, and this reputation had not diminished in 1974 when I began my college career there.

During my second week at school – the first week of September 1974 – President Ford granted his former boss Richard Nixon a full presidential pardon for abuses of power connected with the Watergate scandal. We were aghast, and angry. A protest march was organized. More than 2,000 students marched on the state capitol building. Cars were flipped. An American flag was burned. We were a part of it.

Not only were we part of the march, but my roommate grabbed the American flag that was smoldering on the capitol steps and brought it back to our dorm room. We displayed it on our wall. That week in *Newsweek* magazine, there was an article on the protest in Madison and it mentioned the flag. We looked at it hanging on our wall with pride.

Welcome to Madison, kids.

Party, the Verb

When I hear the word "party" I still think of birthday cake. But it was us Baby Boomers that turned the word "party" into a verb. While the noun "party" still is used to describe an event where people get together to celebrate or have a good time, "to party" means to get high, drunk, stoned or somehow inebriated, usually with others. You're welcome.

For my group of friends, partying was as much a part of college life as going to class, studying, eating and sleeping. Unlike most students, however, we were not into drinking. In fact, we looked down on the drunken frat boys, jocks and other sloppy, slurring and stumbling students who ended up vomiting in hallways, bathrooms and stair wells across campus. That was not cool. Doing drugs was much cooler.

Unlike most of the students I met, I didn't do any drugs in high school except smoke pot. Actually, there was one exception.

The first time I did an illegal drug of any kind was before I'd even had a can of beer or smoked a joint. I was maybe 12 or 13 when my sisters gave me a Quaalude. We were at a restaurant called R.J. Grunt's in Chicago, across from Lincoln Park. It was the first of the "Lettuce Entertain You" restaurants, which became a successful chain of "hip" restaurants in the Chicago area.

At Grunts, they served exotic fare like vegie sandwiches on multigrain bread, homemade potato chips and a creative mix of burgers. The menus looked hand-drawn, with clever names for each item and folksy descriptions. These kinds of places soon became common, but this was brand-new then.

Shortly after we sat down, before we ordered, my sisters asked me if I wanted a Quaalude. They were each going to take one – or a half of one. They said it was pretty strong. I didn't know what a Quaalude was but I said sure, I'll take one.

My sisters suggested I just take a half, which I did. Then when nothing seemed to be happening, I decided to take the other half. My sisters didn't seem to think it was a big deal, as I don't remember them trying hard to stop me.

This was on an empty stomach. Before the food got there, the room began to spin. I began to sway to try to keep up with it. My sisters were kind of laughing at first, but then I guess it got to be too much and they got me outside and took me across the street to the park. I never did anything like that again before college.

The day I moved into the dorm, after saying goodbye to my parents, while Jeff and I are unpacking our stuff, he pulls out several bags of marijuana. He didn't know yet that I smoked. I think he was looking for my reaction.

We immediately bonded and were soon joined by his two best friends from Appleton, Tom and Jim. I then introduced them to my friend Rick, one of only three other people from my high school class to go to Madison. Rick and I were not close in high school, but we got to know each other better senior year when we learned we were both going to Madison.

The five of us got stoned together, then headed down State Street – the main drag leading from campus to Capitol Square – to a "head shop" called Pipefitters. Head shops were very popular in the '70s, kids. They openly sold all kinds of drug paraphernalia. The five of us went in on a 40-inch bamboo bong.

Rick, who played the guitar, volunteered his guitar case to tote the bong to the various parties going on that night in the dorms. We'd show up at someone's door and they'd get excited thinking we were bringing a guitar. Then they'd get more excited when we opened the case and displayed the bong. People would inevitably fill it and we'd be kings of the party.

It wasn't long before I was introduced to other drugs. One, of course, was "speed" or amphetamines. We would do this to stay up all night and study, but being up all night meant we would usually end up partying as well.

Another was MDMA, or what they call Ecstasy today. This too was kind of speedy, but produced a more "euphoric" high. I remember the first time I did it telling the guy who got it for us – a guy named Dan who lived on our floor – that I loved him.

We didn't do much cocaine in college. I recall it was prohibitively expensive compared to other drugs at the time. I did it some after college but never did it much.

The most mind-altering drugs we did – mind-blowing in some cases – were "psychedelics." These included Psilocybin mushrooms and a variety of man-made hallucinogens, including LSD (Lysergic Acid Diethylamide), which we just called "acid."

The first time I did acid was before a showing of the movie *Reefer Madness* on campus. Jeff and I were getting high and rolling a few joints to bring to the show (you could smoke pot pretty openly back then at movies, concerts and other venues) when he casually said he was going to "drop" a hit of acid. Did I want to join him?

Specifically, he was going to ingest a hit of "window pane," which looked like a tiny chip of plastic. It was smaller than the size of a "chad" you'd punch out from a paper voting ballot. It is amazing how something so small could be so powerful.

It started coming on in the middle of *Reefer Madness*. In the dark auditorium, the effects seemed muted at first. My vision got a little blurry. My mind had trouble following the movie. I felt physically speedy. That's all I remember till we got back to our dorm room.

When we got back, Jeff began waving his arms to see if I saw trails. I did. We started smoking pot and maybe even drinking a little to try to take the edge off, but at this point my mind went into overdrive on the most bizarre of thoughts.

It is almost pointless to describe an acid trip to someone who has never been on one. The closest I can come is this: You know how sometimes when you're dreaming, things make sense in the dream that don't make sense in real life? Well, when you're tripping, those kinds of thoughts and scenarios make sense while you're awake, and your actual physical surroundings seem strange and incongruous.

For example, we had an electric frying pan in our room. It looked extremely squat and square and out of place to us. We began laughing at it and couldn't stop. We're laughing and pointing at this thing for no reason other than how strange it looked to us. It almost looked alive, with a face, sort of like Sponge Bob Square Pants if he were an electric frying pan. I was actually expecting it to somehow respond to us. I think it did.

My acids trips lasted forever, like 10 hours or more sometimes. I can see how someone on a so-called "bad" acid trip might totally freak out. This never happened to me. But I could see how it could.

I did acid no more than 10 times while I was in college. For me, it was the mother of all drugs. No, actually, it was the mother fucker of all drugs.

If you've never tried it, I do not recommend it. While, in retrospect, I enjoyed most of my trips, I also recall the near-terror of not being in control of myself or my mind. It was fun but also scary. I never did it again after college.

"Live from New York, It's Saturday Night"

On October 11, 1975, *Saturday Night Live* debuted on NBC television. I didn't see it. I didn't have a TV my first two years of college. My sophomore year at Madison I shared a second-floor apartment in an old converted three-story house off-campus with my freshman-year roommate Jeff and another guy.

Apparently I wasn't alone in not seeing much of *SNL*'s early episodes. The first month or so of the show, they actually repeated several bits, assuming no one had seen them the first time.

I probably started watching *SNL* later that first season when I came home for Thanksgiving or Christmas break. What was I doing those nights? Getting high with my friends from high school? Or getting high with my sisters and their husbands in my parents' basement after they went to bed?

Whenever it was, I'm sure I didn't realize I was watching a show that would establish new standards for television comedy.

The first episode featured George Carlin as host. Most of the hosts the first few seasons were the young, hip comedians and comedic actors of that time. Others included Robert Klein,

Rob Reiner, Richard Pryor, Dick Cavett, Elliott Gould, Buck Henry, Lily Tomlin, and soon-to-be megastar, Steve Martin.

The seven "Not Ready For Prime Time Players" that first season were Dan Ackroyd, John Belushi, Chevy Chase, Garrett Morris, Jane Curtain, Lorraine Newman and Gilda Radner. Chevy Chase would leave the show after the first year and be replaced by Bill Murray.

During *SNL*'s first season, the world was introduced to Andy Kaufman doing his Mighty Mouse lip synch, Chevy Chase's opening fall and Gilda Radner's "Baba Wawa." Gerald Ford was in the White House and his stereotyped clumsiness and dull-wittedness were lampooned ruthlessly.

John Belushi introduced his Joe Cocker impression along with his Samurai and Bee characters. Who can forget *Weekend Update* with Garrett Morris screaming at the top of his lungs in the "News for the Hard of Hearing" segment? And I was totally in love with Candace Bergen, who hosted the show twice in 1975.

Musical guests the first season included Bill Withers performing "Ain't No Sunshine When She's Gone," Jimmy Cliff singing "The Harder They Come" and Janis Ian introducing "Seventeen." Other performers in the early seasons included George Harrison, Billy Preston, Carly Simon, Simon and Garfunkel, Jackson Brown, the Kinks and Frank Zappa.

The segments on pop culture parodied the hot topics of the time. The Patty Hearst trial began during that first season. The U.S. was preparing to convert to the metric system. Claudine Longet got away with murder. The 1976 presidential race was starting to heat up. The movie *Jaws* had been a blockbuster hit that summer. All of these were lampooned on the show.

The "Not Ready for Prime Time Players" weren't much older than I was. This was *my* generation. These people wore their hair like me, did drugs like me, shared the same counter-culture, anti-establishment humor that I did, and were now sharing it with the rest of the world on network television.

This was *our* show, fellow Boomers. It was created by *our* generation. It was *our* kind of humor. Making fun of the establishment. Cheering drug use. Short of *SCTV*, a show out of Canada featuring young comic actors like John Candy and Eugene Levy, and a few bad spinoffs, *SNL* was unique.

And it became the king of cool. Mick Jagger would just show up with Peter Tosh singing reggae. Stars of all kinds now wanted to host. The show still held to a rather closed list at first, with people like Elliott Gould, Steve Martin, Eric Idle, Buck Henry and others hosting over and over again. But by the second season, people like NFL quarterback Fran Tarkenton, television producer Norman Lear, consumer advocate Ralph Nadar, actresses Karen Black and Sissy Spacek, and a range of other celebrities began hosting.

If you hosted *SNL*, you were hip. At that time, the entertainment industry still, for the most part, was not. When we grew up in the '50s and '60s, variety shows and sitcoms on TV were so lame, yet people like my parents still laughed. I couldn't figure out why they thought entertainers like Bob Hope, George Burns, Jack Benny and Milton Berle were funny. I felt this way about all the stars of that era, of my parents' generation.

We Boomers were between our late teens and early 30s when *SNL* premiered and made pointed political and social satire okay to put on TV. Our parents didn't watch it. We did. It catered to our tastes, our ability to bust-open certain taboos and dare people to find something wrong with it – and make it funny. To laugh at the Establishment that was still in control but that we'd soon be taking over.

We're now in our 50s and 60s and *SNL* is still on the air. There aren't many television shows that have been on my entire adult life. (Reruns don't count.) It isn't our show anymore. The guest hosts and musical guests are no longer of our generation, and 11:30 p.m. Eastern is now past most of our bedtimes. But I, for one, remember and cherish the comedy that came from that show during those early seasons. For all of us, I believe it was part of our coming of age.

Zappa

One of the early episodes of *Saturday Night Live* that was hosted by Candace Bergen featured musical guest Frank Zappa. I had actually met Frank Zappa earlier that year when he did a concert in Madison.

I had been home in Chicago for the weekend and was driving back to Madison on Sunday. Zappa was scheduled to play that night at the Dane County Coliseum. My roommate Jeff and I had tickets.

I stopped for gas in Beloit, Wisconsin, about halfway between Chicago and Madison. As I approached the ramp to get back on the interstate, I saw a young woman with a backpack hitch-hiking. I picked her up.

She said she was going to the Zappa concert. She asked if I was. I told her that, as a matter of fact, I was.

"I'm bringing this to Frank," she said, unzipping her backpack and pulling out what looked like about a pound of marijuana.

"Fuck!" I said. "Please put that away!"

"Why, don't you smoke?" she asked.

"Yes, I do, I just don't want to get busted!"

I think I was still on supervision for my pot bust in high school due to our inept lawyer. I was paranoid driving with that much pot in the car. I got even more paranoid when she started rolling a joint and asked if I wanted to get high.

She rolled what she called a "pregnant bear." It was a joint with a big bud in the middle that bulged out.

The pot was good. I got real stoned. Of course, it was for Frank fucking Zappa, assuming this broad was telling the truth.

When we got to Madison, I dropped her off at her hotel and went home to tell Jeff. He went nuts when I told him what I'd done.

"Are you crazy?" he exclaimed. "You dropped her off at her hotel? How could you do that? We could have met Frank Zappa!"

I wasn't a big Frank Zappa fan. Meeting him was not a big deal to me. But it was to Jeff.

"Let's go find her," he said. "Let's go meet Frank Zappa."

We went back to the hotel, and amazingly enough, the girl I picked up was still in the lobby. She lit up when she saw us walk in.

"I am so glad to see you," she said to me. "Frank is at the Coliseum rehearsing and I don't have a ride there. Can you take me?"

I said sure, introduced her to Jeff, and the three of us headed to the Coliseum. We pulled up in back and she got out to talk to the security guard. A few seconds later, she motions for us to wait and disappears into the building, backpack and all, which they never checked (this would never happen today). It was still hours before the show.

A few minutes later, she came out, sans backpack, and motioned for us to come in. The next thing I knew, I'm on the stage of the Coliseum with Frank Zappa and the Mothers of Invention rehearsing right in front of me.

They stopped playing and the girl introduced me as the guy who drove her from Beloit. Frank nodded at me appreciatively. Then he began barking at me like a dog.

I guess that was supposed to be keeping in character with the wacky, zany, crazy persona Frank Zappa had cultivated in the rock world. I'd have rather smoked a joint with him.

Actually, I probably could have, but we blew it. After they wrapped up rehearsing, we were allowed to hang out in the wings till the show started. We remained there through the opening band – the Climax Electric Blues Band or something like that – sitting on these giant amps through most of the show. But we couldn't really see and the sound wasn't as good there so we went down into the crowd like idiots for Zappa. When we wanted to go back on stage, they wouldn't let us.

No lessons here, fellow Boomers. I just wanted to share my Frank Zappa story.

The Bicentennial

In 1976, the United States celebrated its 200th birthday. The Bicentennial saw towns across America paint themselves red, white and blue and host patriotic events. There was a national Bicentennial logo and slews of corporate sponsorships. Everyone, it seemed, was wrapping themselves in the flag.

Not all of us were feeling that patriotic, however. A Republican was still in the White House. The Vietnam War, Watergate and Ford's pardon of Nixon were still fresh in our minds. The commercialization of the Bicentennial was over the top, leading some to call it the "Buy Centennial."

What I remember as most galling, however, was President Ford aligning himself with and virtually taking ownership of the Bicentennial in an election year. His Democratic challenger in the fall election would not be determined until after the July 4 celebration, and he took full advantage.

Ford wanted people to associate his presidency with the restoration of America's pride and confidence. He made speeches at famous Revolutionary War sites, hosted nationally televised entertainment events, and appeared at local festivals.

He made the Bicentennial the focus of his early, unofficial reelection campaign.

To us, Ford was a dim-witted Republican – a member of the Warren Commission no less – who wasn't even elected, but became president only because the guy who appointed him vice president resigned in disgrace. And that guy was Nixon, whom Ford subsequently pardoned in what we were sure was a pre-arranged deal.

The 1976 election would be the first time I'd be eligible to vote. I was firmly behind Jimmy Carter, the eventual Democratic nominee, as were all my left-leaning, righty-hating friends. We watched the debates (I had a TV by then), laughing at Ford with as biased a viewpoint as you might expect from stoned college students who couldn't wait to erase the stench of the Nixon years from the White House.

Carter won in November. We were happy about that. But the summer of 1976 was one to remember.

Bicentennial-mania was most visible in the many small towns that dot our country from coast to coast. There were small-town festivals – real "mom, apple pie and hurray for the red, white and blue" kinds of happenings – all summer long.

I got a chance to see some of this up close. Straight from the files of "How I Spent my Summer Vacation," I spent the summer of 1976 selling encyclopedias door-to-door in small towns across three states in the Midwest.

It was that or spend the summer between my sophomore and junior year of college back at my parents' house in Skokie. Rather than get a "real" job, I settled for one where they would take any warm body because your pay was strictly commission: $100 for every set of encyclopedias sold.

It was the ultimate "Hated it at the time, love it in retrospect" experience. Considering I sold only six sets of encyclopedias in six weeks, you can imagine how much rejection I endured. Yet, I look back on it with mostly fond memories.

The first three weeks, I went door-to-door in small towns in Wisconsin. I was part of a three-person crew. My other crew members were Sue, an attractive blond around my age but not a student – this was her full-time job – and Natalie, a strong and outgoing 30-ish woman who also was the boss's wife.

Other crews were mostly male and four people rather than three. I think I got put on a crew with Sue and Natalie because they liked me. The crews would meet each afternoon at the Collier office in downtown Madison. These were Collier encyclopedias. We'd all practice our spiels on each other and then head out in our crews to our respective towns.

Usually, each member of the crew got dropped off in a different town. These were very small towns, so you were basically expected to cover the whole town from late afternoon until dark. Dark was either 9 or 10 p.m. depending what time zone you were in, Central or Eastern (Wisconsin was Central).

At the end of the night, you were supposed to go to a designated pick-up point, which was usually the local tavern. All these towns seemed to have one particular bar where the locals would meet. There were some nights I got so frustrated with doors being slammed in my face, or I just didn't feel like selling, that I'd just go straight to the bar and drink with the locals till I got picked up.

I don't recall if I sold anything those first three weeks. Most of the time, I never made it past the front door. The first time I remember being invited in it was by a group of teenagers partying at someone's parents' house. Technically, I was not allowed to enter a home unless both the male and female heads of the household were there, but shit, this looked like fun.

One of the girls was particularly attractive and seemed real interested, either in me or my encyclopedias or both. Yes, these were teenagers, but I was only 20. Unfortunately, she looked to be about eight months pregnant. She sat attentively through my sales pitch, though, and scolded others when they tried to interrupt.

Another time, a woman told me her husband was at work but she really wanted to hear about the encyclopedias. Again, I was not supposed to go in without a husband and wife present (which is crazy given all the single parents) but I did anyway. The woman immediately put on music, which was very distracting while I was trying to do my presentation. Then her husband barges in and throws me out.

The most fun was at the pick-up points. Usually, by the time I got there, everyone in town knew who I was. "That's the salesman," they'd mutter, having seen me knocking on doors all night. They'd buy me drinks and I'd get incredibly loaded at these watering holes. I didn't have to drive, so what the hell? I wouldn't get home till about 2 a.m. and then do the same thing in another town the next day.

After three weeks of doing small towns in Wisconsin, I was told to pack for a one-week road trip to Indiana or Michigan, I don't remember which. It doesn't matter because it ended up being a three-week trip to both Indiana *and* Michigan.

Another crew joined Natalie, Sue and I as we headed first to Indiana. Two other crews, being driven by Natalie's husband, would meet us there the next day. We had to pay for our own motel rooms, although we slept four to a room and we stayed in dives, so it wasn't too bad cost-wise.

The drive to Indiana was long. I ended up making out in the back seat with this girl from the other crew that was riding with us (I've chosen to withhold her name).

That night, I slept with this girl in the girls' room with Sue and Natalie in the next bed. I couldn't believe they didn't hear us. We learned later that they did, they were just too embarrassed to move.

They ultimately sent this girl home, which was fine with me, as she was becoming a pain in the ass. But I had earned new-found respect from the male members of the other crews when they learned of all this.

"That is so great that you fucked her, man," they'd say, offering me another beer.

My best night selling was in St. Joseph, Michigan, when I sold two sets of encyclopedias in one night. Remember, I only sold six sets in six weeks, so this was one-third of my whole summer's take. To top it off, the couple that bought the second set, after giving me their deposit check, invited me to stay and do bongs with them. It was a great night.

There were other interesting experiences. I learned that in many of these towns, all the households seemed to be in the hands of babysitters on Saturday nights. I got invited in by a few, and took them up on it, which was absolutely taboo. I attended community softball games, where it seemed everyone in town was there. There were town cook-outs and parades. This was small-town America during the Bicentennial. It was great to experience.

On the whole, though, I wouldn't wish door-to-door encyclopedia sales on my worst enemy. I quit immediately upon returning to Madison after the road trip.

Jeff was sitting on the front porch sipping wine when they dropped me off. It was around 6 in the morning. Ah, youth.

Turns out he'd been up all night, as had I, but not having seen each other for three weeks, we decided to forego sleep and party. He had this homemade wine and we drank and smoked pot while I told him all about my trip. I also told him I planned to quit; that I had knocked on my last door for Collier's.

Then we hopped in the car and decided to drive to New Glarus. It was a wine-and-cheese town and they were having some Sunday family day for the Bicentennial. The whole town was decked out in red, white and blue. Even the curbs and fire hydrants had been painted.

We spent the rest of the day walking all around New Glarus, drinking more wine and smoking more pot. As dusk settled, we figured it was time to head back to Madison. We were both so sleep-deprived, we're lucky we made it back.

At the house, there was a letter waiting for me (yes kids, sent snail mail) from the girl I slept with on the road trip. She said how she was looking forward to renewing our "relationship" when I returned to Madison. What relationship? I saw her a couple more times and that was it.

Postscript: In 1982 – six years later and four years after I graduated – I returned to Madison for a visit and stopped at a pizza place for lunch. My waitress was this girl. I don't think she recognized me. If she did, she sure didn't show it. I pretended I didn't recognize her. She was very pregnant. I never used a condom when we slept together but that was six years ago. Still, it made me think. Was this her only child? I really didn't want to know.

End of the Boom

I 'm going to wrap this up rather quickly because once we got into the 1980s, we started turning into our parents. That's where the nostalgia ends for me, folks.

Some of us made a lot of money and went on to do great things. Most of us have simply done our best to eke out careers, raise families, feel happy and fulfilled, and most recently, start preparing for retirement.

I graduated from Wisconsin in 1978 with a degree in journalism. The highlight of my college journalism career was covering Vice President Robert Dole's visit to Madison during the Carter-Ford presidential election.

As a reporter for the *Daily Cardinal*, UW-Madison's student newspaper, I was assigned to cover Dole's speech at an exclusive Republican event. I arrived in my grungy jeans, untucked shirt and giant afro with backpack, camera and note pad. Secret Service agents immediately ushered me into a tiny room and grilled me on who I was and why I was there. After a call to my editor and many dirty looks, they finally released me to mix with the slimy, well-dressed crowd.

I had five jobs my first six years after college. I did corporate communications work — speech writing, press releases, employee publications, annual reports, video scripts and other organizational propaganda. (Hey, I had to make a living.)

In 1983, I was working as an "editor at large" for the American Bar Association Press in Chicago when *Today's Chicago Woman* magazine named me one of the "25 Most Eligible Bachelors in Chicago." The other bachelors included Reggie Theus of the Chicago Bulls, Bob Avellini of the Chicago Bears, and 22 guys you never heard of. They had a large reception for us at Chicago's Hyatt Regency hotel. For one night I felt what it was like to be a celebrity. It was a fun night.

I was 24 when the 1980s arrived. Ronald Reagan was elected president that year. At the time, it was my worst nightmare. I was still the liberal Boomer who discovered social conscious-ness in the 60s and ingrained it in myself in the 70s. I thought the same way in the 80s. I still do.

Actually, Reagan didn't turn out as bad as I feared. I thought with his chest-thumping, hawkish, Old West bravado he would start World War III. That didn't happen.

HOWEVER, in almost every other way, I considered the Rea-gan presidency a disaster. It is where a lot of us Boomers went our separate ways. It spawned a reversal in the country from increasingly liberal ideals to a new conservatism. It was as if all the consciousness-raising and new ways of thinking we introduced in the 60s and 70s was wiped out.

Money, materialism and greed were back in vogue and bigger than ever. America's military industrial complex went into high gear, fueled by Reagan's desire to replenish our weapons arsenals and flex our military muscles more aggressively to regain lost respect in the world.

Spending was cut in almost every other category and taxes were reduced. One area where spending was not cut was the "war on drugs." Reagan made that a priority. His wife's "Just Say No" campaign dashed the hopes of those of us who craved a more intelligent drug policy – like one that does not view use as a crime, but abuse as a health issue.

Reagan's strong appeal to evangelical Christians was also unsettling. This is probably as good a place as any to tell you that I believe organized religion is the biggest fraud perpetrated on mankind. I also believe everyone has a right to believe what they want to believe. But whatever you believe, it is hard to argue that few things are more divisive than religion.

The combination of how seriously people take their religion and there not being one universally accepted religion creates a powder keg of biblical proportions. One's religion should provide one comfort. Yet it seems the more religious someone is, the more militant they are toward those who believe differently. It is amazing to me that in the 21st century there are still people that feel justified in killing other people who don't share their religious beliefs as a means to please their imaginary gods. I believe generations from now they'll look back on religion as another element of a still-primitive society.

Most distressing to me about of the emergence of the "New Right" was that Boomers made up so much of it. They flocked to the Sun Belt, not just for the weather, but where jobs in the defense industry were abundant under Reagan. They liked making money and hating paying taxes, which fit perfectly with "Reaganomics."

What happened?!?

I thought it was a good sign when Jimmy Carter was elected president in 1976. I liked him. I thought he was a good, honest man of high principles. I thought he was well-intentioned. He wasn't corrupt (which, so soon after Nixon, was no small consideration). I thought he was very intelligent and progressive in his thinking.

Unfortunately, two things did him in: inflation and the Iran Hostage Crisis, mostly the latter. Many Democrats switched over to vote for Reagan in the 1980 election because they viewed Carter as weak due to his inability to bring the hostages home after more than a year in captivity. Reagan's tough talk and vow to cut taxes to rein in inflation was the perfect tonic for the country at the time.

To refresh your memory, or for those of you who still weren't born yet, in November 1979, Iranian students stormed the U.S. Embassy in Tehran and took more than 60 Americans hostage. They hated the U.S. and Carter for allowing the deposed and dying Shah of Iran into the U.S. for cancer treatment. There was no negotiating with these captors. In April 1980, Carter tried a heroic rescue attempt, but it went badly awry, further reducing the president's standing.

The November 1980 election marked more than a year since the hostages were taken. Carter barely campaigned for reelection, focusing all his energies on the hostage situation. Reagan took full advantage, telling people if he was president and Iran didn't release the hostages, there would be no more Iran.

Such incendiary talk would be irresponsible for the president, but it did wonders for candidate Reagan. He won the election easily. On the day of his inauguration, just hours after his speech, the hostages were released. The man was a hero.

Some have speculated that Iran released the hostages because they were afraid of what Reagan might do upon taking office. Others claimed Reagan had a secret deal with Iran not to release the hostages until after the election. Still others thought Iran simply wanted to embarrass Carter.

Reagan made good on his promise to cut taxes. The largest cuts went to wealthy individuals and corporations. The idea, still adhered to by Republicans today, is that by making the rich richer, they will hire, spend and invest more, with the financial benefits of all that "trickling down" to the rest of us. Despite studies disproving this theory, many people still buy it.

Reagan's economic policies sank the country into its worst recession since the Great Depression. With insufficient tax revenue to fund his agenda (guess things weren't "trickling down" fast enough), he borrowed heavily, creating record budget deficits. When his successor, George H.W. Bush, raised taxes to try to undo some of the damage, he was booted out of office. It took Bill Clinton to finally clean up the mess, leaving us with a record budget *surplus* upon leaving office. Of course, this was subsequently squandered by his successor, George W. Bush. We may never recover from that presidency.

Despite all this, Reagan maintained high approval ratings throughout his presidency and Republicans still hold him up as one of the great presidents of our time. This absolutely boggles my mind.

In addition to Reagan's election, the early 1980s saw assassinations take center stage again with the deaths of Beatle John Lennon and Egyptian President Anwar Sadat, and the attempt on Reagan's life by would-be assassin John Hinkley. It almost felt like 1968 all over again.

Acquired Immune Deficiency Syndrome (AIDS), a deadly sexually transmitted disease that still has no cure, surfaced during the Reagan years. It sent shock waves through the gay community, since homosexuals were its most common early victims. Some people on the Right considered AIDS to be God's punishment for the sin of being a homosexual.

On the positive side, we got cool technologies like VCRs and CDs in the 1980s. The former actually allowed us to tape TV shows and play them later when it was convenient, even speeding through the commercials. This was a huge deal, kids.

Of course, VCRs were soon obsoleted by DVD players. Then "on demand" television completely re-wrote the TV viewing playbook.

I still have a few VHS tapes and a VCR/DVD combo unit if I ever want to play them. It's as if I can't completely let go of that technology.

As for CDs, I remember as if it were yesterday walking into a record store in the mid-1980s and being blindsided by the complete absence of vinyl records. They had all been replaced by smaller disks called CDs.

I admit I had not attempted to buy any new music the few years prior. I was busy getting engaged, moving from the city to the suburbs, getting married, having kids and taking out a mortgage. Life was moving fast. I'd heard of CDs, I just had no idea they had completely replaced vinyl. My turntable was now obsolete, forcing me to buy a CD player.

A short time later, we got our first cell phone. It was the size of a brick and almost as heavy. The first time I used it, I took it with me when I took the kids to lunch at Denny's. We're sitting at a table in the middle of the restaurant when it starts ringing. I had no idea how to answer it. I'm looking for something that says "answer" or "pick up" or something. Long story short, it kept ringing and ringing, causing great embarrassment as I searched for a way to answer the damn thing.

I have welcomed the advancements in cell phones since the "brick" days. I've accepted that cameras no longer need film to take pictures. I've accepted that you don't even need cameras any more since they're now built into every phone. I even appreciate things like text messaging and being able to access email and the Internet on my phone. But is there anyone else like me who feels like shouting "Enough Already!"?

I realize that some of us Baby Boomers have grasped willingly every technological advance that's come to us in our lifetimes. But I am one of those newly minted curmudgeons that have had enough. I'm all for progress. But I have no desire to watch a sporting event on the two-inch screen of my phone. I do not need to be in constant contact with the world. I actually prefer the world to leave me alone.

Cell phones were something we didn't seem to anticipate when we were growing up in the 1960s. In Stanley Kubrick's 1969 film, *2001: A Space Odyssey*, the latest phone technology was the "picture phone" where you could see the person you're talking to. (Or as my daughter says, "You mean like Face Time?") But it was still a "landline." No one imagined portable phones.

So, now we can carry our phones around and they can do a lot of stuff. Great. My kids laugh at me for not using 90 percent of the functions available on my phone. But I am at peace. I need no more technology. Please.

I got married in 1984. I met my first wife at my second job after college, in 1980, although we lost touch for a couple of years in between. Our wedding was in the famous Purple Hotel in Lincolnwood, Illinois, abutting Chicago's north side.

The Purple Hotel was a Chicago landmark. Owned by Hyatt, it was called the Lincolnwood Hyatt when it opened in 1960 and soon became one of Chicago's hottest night spots. The biggest stars in entertainment stayed there when they played Chicago. Michael Jordon, after being drafted by the Bulls in 1984, spent his first night in Chicago there, just months before my wedding.

The hotel was both famous and infamous. In 1983, Allan Dorfman – a reputed Chicago mobster – was gunned down in the hotel's parking lot. He had been convicted of conspiring to bribe a U.S. senator and faced more than 50 years in prison.

Some have speculated he was killed to keep him from divulging mob secrets in exchange for a lighter sentence. The crime has never been solved.

That same year, a plumbing executive also was murdered at the hotel. In that case, a disgruntled employee of the victim's plumbing firm was found to have done him in. These incidents took place a year before my wedding.

The hotel came to be known as the Purple Hotel because it was, well, purple. It's been said that it was originally supposed to be blue but the brick supplier shipped the wrong color bricks.

My sister Michele also got married there, in January 1967. Exactly 40 years later, mold, rats and other code violations forced the hotel to close. It sat vacant, becoming a rusting purple eyesore, for six more years before a wrecking ball turned the Chicago landmark into a pile of rubble in 2013.

My son was born in 1986. His sister was born in 1988. *Captain Kangaroo*, Haight Ashbury and UW-Madison all began to seem very far away. For the next 20 years, I was the sole breadwinner in my household, forcing me out of my comfort zone in an attempt to make enough money to provide all of us a nice life and send my kids to college. Fatherhood became my primary focus.

For all intents and purposes, the Baby Boom years were over. A new generation, called the Millennials, was getting ready to take the reins.

As I said in the beginning, it's been a great ride. We grew up during a time of great change and we had a major impact – in politics, pop culture and society at large.

Not all of us did drugs, took part in protest marches, and dodged the draft. Not all of us changed our ways of thinking from that of our parents. Not all of us developed and maintained liberal ideals born of those turbulent years.

That was my circle. That was my experience. But I was just one of 80 million. The older I get, the more I realize it really doesn't matter, at least not anymore. We Boomers are a dying breed. We should just try to enjoy ourselves for what little time we have left. Shouldn't we?

Now, quit Bogarting that joint.

Epilogue

As I said in the Prologue, nearly 80 million Baby Boomers were born between 1946 and 1964. At our peak, we made up 40 percent of the U.S. population. Today, we make up about 25 percent.

Unfortunately (for us), this percentage will continue to decline as we continue to age and die out over the next 50 years. Ironically, the generation that pushed to end discrimination is now being discriminated against. I'm talking about age discrimination. Yes, this is happening. We're losing jobs and not getting re-hired.

We are now the older generation.

Being born in 1955 put me smack-dab in the middle of the Baby Boom. But that doesn't make me your "typical" Boomer because I don't think there is such thing. I hope at least some of what I've related in these pages resonates with those of you who lived during this time. And for you youngsters out there, maybe you've learned a little about our generation, albeit from one person's first-hand account.

I think we did some great things. I think inroads made by minorities (we do have an African American president), the gay community (there is finally gay marriage) and others who have been denied equal rights can be attributed at least in part to some of our social consciousness-raising in the 1960s. Of course, we still have a long way to go.

No one can doubt the contributions we made to music. My son, a musician himself, says he envies me for growing up when I did because of the music that emerged in that era. I know what he means. And I am grateful.

Also, as I've more than alluded to, I'm a little disappointed that the liberal direction we seemed headed in the 60s seemed to stop abruptly and reverse itself in the 1980s. I regret that we Baby Boomers were unable to unite under a more liberal political ideology moving forward. But I rue even more how divided we are now in this country. I didn't see that coming.

Of course, it is hard to coexist peacefully when you have a political system that pits two sides against each other so fiercely. Our two-party system boils down a myriad of disparate beliefs into two monolithic entities that define who we are and compete like they're each trying to win the Super Bowl. They don't even show good sportsmanship, disparaging the other side at every turn. How are we supposed to stand united as a country when our own system tears us apart?

I know I tend to disparage "Republicans" as if each one of the millions of people who happen to vote for this party over the other is stupid or greedy or evil or worse. This is ridiculous. Most people vote based on their self-interest or whatever their "hot button" issue is. I have a friend who always votes for the candidate he perceives as most pro-Israel, regardless of party or positions on other issues. I know someone else who votes Republican because she believes its economic policies are more beneficial to her and to American business, yet she is pro-choice.

"It's still the best damn system in the world," our blindly patriotic brethren say without thinking, believing that everything in this country is better than anywhere else. This is another reason change is so hard to come by in this country.

Take our nation's health care system ... please. One thing I have in common with Republicans is that I too hate Obamacare. But we hate it for different reasons. I hate it because it is far more complex and costly than a single-payer national health care system would be. Republicans hate it simply because it is complex and costly, and because it is this president's signature piece of legislation.

Let's back up. In 1994, I went into business for myself. My previous job had been with a large corporation, through which I had health insurance for me and my family. When I formed my own business, I had to get my own health insurance.

My wife had a pre-existing condition: she was nuts. Seriously, she had anxiety issues for which she'd been prescribed a mild sedative. No insurer would provide me with a family plan that included my wife. The best I could do was to include a rider stating that any services related to my wife's anxiety would not be covered.

This was the world of health care in the United States before Obamacare, folks. Obama's many haters feel this was better than our current system. I'm sorry, but you people are idiots.

In *every other developed country on the face of the earth*, the government pays for health care for its citizens. Only this country insists on keeping health care privatized under the notion that insurance companies, with an objective of maximizing profits, will fund health care more efficiently than the government.

Is Obamacare overly complex, inefficient and costly? Absolutely, because the hoops the Republicans made the president and other Democrats go through to make sure private insurers would still make their profits while no longer denying coverage to people with pre-existing conditions is the reason the system is the way it is. If the Democrats had their druthers, we'd have a single-payer, government-funded national health care system like *every other developed country on the face of the earth*. But Republicans consider this socialism. They can't get past the word.

And while we're at it, we're also the only country that drags employers into the health insurance business, expecting them to subsidize their employees' health care costs. This can't be good for our global competitiveness.

Of course, a single-payer national health care system would mean higher taxes. How else is the government supposed to pay for everyone's health care? What gets lost in the debate is that the taxes should be no more than the premiums we're already paying private insurers, and would probably be less.

When Congress was negotiating the terms of Obamacare, Republicans would not even consider a *public option* for people who could not get coverage from private insurers due to pre-existing conditions. They implied that private insurers would not be able to compete with a not-for-profit govern-ment payer. Isn't this basically admitting you think the gov-ernment can fund health care more efficiently with no profit motive?

Instead, Republicans agreed (reluctantly) that for-profit insur-ers could no longer deny coverage to people with pre-existing conditions as long as everyone was required to buy insurance. Then they complained that forcing people to buy insurance was unconstitutional.

This country spends far more per capita on health care than any other country and our outcomes are no better than mid-dle of the pack. On what basis can we say that our unique style of financing health care is better than everyone else's?

Come on, people. I know you all think we, America, are the best. But there is a reason that *every other developed country on the face of the earth* pays for health care for its citizens. To deny such a thing is inhumane. You can read all the propaganda you want about people waiting in lines in Canada, or people in Europe not getting the quality of services we do. The fact is no country has ever shown any inclination to can its health-care system for ours.

I have friends who are Republicans, believe it or not. Shortly after Obamacare became law, one of them complained that he knew someone whose insurance premiums were going to go up 30 percent "because of Obamacare."

"That's because the insurance companies have to make their profits," I explained. "They used to be able to just insure peo-ple who would be profitable and turn down people who might have actual medical needs. Now they have to insure everybody. So to maintain their profits, they have to raise premiums."

"Well," he said. "All I know is, whenever the government gets involved in something, it gets fucked up."

That's another thing about Republicans. They wave their flags, fawn all over veterans and claim to be patriotic, yet they seem to dislike and mistrust their own government. But see? I've just lumped millions of people in one bucket again. I can't help it. It's the two-party system. If you vote Republican, it means you're against having a single-payer national health care system like *every other developed country on the face of the earth* – even if you're not.

I'll conclude this editorial on health care and politics by pointing out that we already have a government-financed national health care system, folks. It is called Medicare. And soon it will cover the majority of health care expenses in this country. That's because the biggest users of health care, by far, are the elderly. And pretty soon, all of us Boomers – all 25 percent of the population of us – will be elderly and on Medicare. Some of us already are.

Wouldn't it make sense to simply extend Medicare to everyone, adding the young and healthy to pay into the system, and be done with it? Republicans have yet to propose any other alternative short of eliminating Obamacare and going back to the previous system that gave private insurers all the control and millions of Americans being denied coverage. Their silence is telling.

I've got other gripes. I have gone from being a member of the hippie generation to being a crotchety old man.

There is greater disparity than ever between the haves and have-nots. The environment continues to deteriorate while half the world buries their heads in the sand pretending a problem doesn't exist. The racial divide seems incapable of closing. And when the day comes when we have to leave this planet due to some natural or cosmic calamity, will we be able to do so? Most people would say we're lucky if we haven't destroyed ourselves by then.

But then the other side of me says, relax. Quit thinking like a liberal activist, like you're still in Madison in the 70s. It's not your world anymore. Let it go.

I was married to my first wife for 20 years before getting divorced in 2005. In 2010, I married my second wife: the girl who was sitting a few rows in front of me at Kenny Holtz-man's no-hitter in 1969. We are excited about becoming grandparents. Life is good. Honestly, I have never been happier.

I didn't get rich like many of my fellow Boomers did. I have friends who are millionaires. I seem happier than most of them. What does this tell you?

Obviously, it tells you that money isn't the key to happiness. I know you've probably heard that a million times, kids. But I'm living proof that it's true.

I've learned that to be happy you need to be comfortable in your own skin. That means being able to look in the mirror and being proud of what you see. It means leading a life of high morals – real shit like putting others first and being the best parent you can be, not simply reading the Bible and going to church on Sunday.

As for the value of the Baby Boom generation and our contributions to mankind, I'll leave that to the historians. I mean, we're not dead yet, are we?

Yes, our bodies are starting to ache for no reason. We go to bed when we used to go out. We (or at least some of us) live in fear of our money running out. We're starting to say things that don't make sense like our parents did, becoming a source of great amusement to our kids.

Life just cycles on, doesn't it? And through the good graces of a god I don't believe in, it will do so for many more generations to come.

But, as I said before and I'll say it again: Life is a crapshoot, kids. So enjoy it while you can. Don't take things too seriously. Be sure to laugh, cry, love and hurt, because those are all sure signs you're alive.

And thanks for reading. I love you all.